THE SLUMBER OF CHRISTIANITY

Awakening a Passion for Heaven on Earth

Ted Dekker

NELSON BOOKS
A Division of Thomas Nelson Publishers
Since 1798

www.thomasnelson.com

Published in Nashville, Tennessee, by Thomas Nelson, Inc.

Nelson books may be purchased in bulk for educational, business, fundraising, or sales promotional use. For information, please e-mail SpecialMarkets@ThomasNelson.com.

Library of Congress Cataloging-in-Publication Data

Dekker, Ted, 1962-
    The slumber of Christianity : awakening a passion for heaven on earth / Ted Dekker.
      p. cm.
   ISBN 0-7852-1223-X (hardcover)
   1. Revivals. 2. Church renewal. I. Title.
BV3790.D4754 2005
243--dc22   2005008269

Printed in the United States of America

05 06 07 08 QW 5 4 3 2 1

Contents

FOREWORD

Rise up from slumber. Set your mind and heart on an inheritance that will blow your mind. Feel your heart flutter and find a new passion for life here and now. This is the call from Ted Dekker, who writes with passion and insight on the search for happiness and heaven.

"Are you desperately longing for heaven?" It's a question that begs answering. Peter says, "We are looking forward to the new heavens and new earth" (2 Peter 3:13). But, in fact, as Christians today *are* we? Are we actually looking forward to and *longing for* our eternal home?

Heaven plays a major role in my novels and nonfiction. Researching my book *Heaven*, I read 150 volumes on the subject, many long out-of-print. I've taught a seminary course "A Theology of Heaven." I've received literally thousands of letters and e-mails about heaven. There's a great deal I don't know, but one thing I *do* know is what Christians think about heaven. And how *seldom* we think about it.

Sadly, Ted is right when he says "the church today has little passion for the coming life."

What a contrast to the early Christians. Their pictures on the catacomb walls portrayed heaven with beautiful landscapes, children playing, people feasting at banquets. Believers throughout the ages saw heaven as a constant source of strength and perspective. It was their central reference point, the north star by which they navigated their lives. But today, heaven has fallen off our radar screens.

What God made us to desire is exactly what he promises: a resurrected life in resurrected bodies, in a resurrected community, with the resurrected Christ on a resurrected Earth. This is the eternal heaven that awaits us, and should daily capture our imaginations.

Ted's right—we're slumbering. We need to wake up and smell the New Earth. Taste the coming resurrection. The doctrines of resurrection and New Earth mean that this present world, though suffering under sin and curse, is bursting with clues and foretastes of the coming world.

The Carpenter from Nazareth is preparing a place for us. He knows how to build. He's constructed entire worlds, billions of them. He's going to strip the damaged paint off the old Earth, sand and refinish it, then present it magnificent and pristine. He says it will one day be our home . . . and *His*, for He will dwell there with His people, forever bringing heaven to earth (Revelation 21:3).

With the Lord we love and with the friends we cherish, believers will embark together on the ultimate adventure, in a spectacular new universe awaiting our dominion and exploration. Jesus will be the cosmic center. Joy will be the air we breathe.

And right when we think, "It doesn't get any better than this"—*it will*.

So listen to Ted Dekker's wake-up call. You'll never regret the world you'll wake up to . . . not in a billion years.

— RANDY ALCORN,
BEST-SELLING AUTHOR OF *HEAVEN*

PART I

Our Descent into Slumber

1

The Slumber of Christianity

The Death of Our Dreams

John is forty years old and by all earthly standards a successful man. He's happily married, has raised four children, and
owns a landscaping company that easily affords him a comfortable life. He's also a godly man as best I can tell.

We leaned against his blue Ford F150 in my driveway after
discussing what trees would look best in my backyard. Dusk
was upon us. I took a breath and sprang a question I've asked
many godly men lately.

"Do you ever feel like all you do is work for a payday that
never seems to arrive?"

He adjusted his Rockies baseball cap and looked at me past
graying brows. I knew immediately that the question had struck
a chord. Not surprising—the question always strikes a chord. I
pushed further.

"I mean, think about it. Has your payday ever really arrived?"

"No, not really," he said.

"But you have money. A decent life . . ."

"Sure."

"So what does it take to find true happiness?" I asked.
"You've lived the life, so tell me. How does someone like me
find satisfaction?"

He thought a moment and then looked at the horizon intro-
spectively. "In the small things. A good marriage, a good family,

a good job. And church, of course. A relationship with God. In the end, that's what counts."

"How's that?"

"This world hands us all kinds of challenges, and without God's strength I don't think we stand a chance. Like they say, his strength is made perfect in our weakness. That's the key to happiness."

"But your ship has never come in, so to speak," I said. "Life is mostly a struggle. No big payday yet. It's always just around the corner; am I right?"

"Well . . . I guess. I don't really know what—"

"You ever see *The Matrix*, John?" I interrupted.

"Sure. Good movie."

"What if we're asleep, like Neo was in *The Matrix*?" I asked. "What if the reason we can't find any lasting satisfaction in life is because we're all asleep to a truth that would change our lives forever?"

"That's the advantage Christians have," he said. "That's what I'm saying."

"No, John. What if *Christians* are asleep? What if we're missing the point of our lives here on earth? What if the church is asleep to a truth that would wake us from a deep slumber? Ever think about that?"

John just stared at me.

But that didn't surprise me either. Christians often just stare at me when I first talk to them about the slumber of Christianity.

The Slumber

John is the victim of a slumber that holds hundreds of millions of Christians in the dark, unaware of their own demise.

Perhaps you know of this slumber; perhaps you don't. Either way, any living soul who is even remotely concerned with enjoying life this side of death needs to know about a terrible short-sightedness that has lulled Christians by the millions into a deep sleep. Their life in God simply isn't as thrilling as it once was, and they've settled for that disappointment.

At its very roots, Christianity is a faith that once loudly proclaimed hope for the downtrodden and a staggering dream of great reward for all who believed. But in the epic battle over mankind's souls, the dream of eternity's bliss has been buried in the rubble of misguided teaching. The stunning dreams we once all dreamed have become casualties of war.

The Rolling Stones had it right: *I can't get no satisfaction. Though I try and I try and I try . . . I can't get no satisfaction.*

I would add another phrase: *Even though I'm a Christian, I can't get no satisfaction. Though I try, and I try, and I try, I can't get no satisfaction.*

The band U2 cried out in their *Joshua Tree* album: *But I still haven't found what I'm looking for.*

I would add more: *I go to church; I've been forgiven for my sins, but I still haven't found what I'm looking for.*

Have you ever wondered what happened to the dream that once urged you forward without regard for how difficult the path might become?

> Have you ever wondered what happened to the dream that once urged you forward without regard for how difficult the path might become?

Have you ever wondered why you no longer approach life with the giddy happiness that once possessed you as a child? Think back to those early grade-school years, when the simple fact that it was Friday sent a thrill through your mind. Saturday was coming, and the adventure set before you was enough to make the last few classes drift by in a hazy blur.

Think back to the days leading up to your birthday, when all you could think about was the day you would be king or queen for a few hours. There would be a party and a cake and a new bike or a new doll to celebrate.

Think back to the weeks leading up to Christmas. Your anticipation for that final hour when you would tear into the packages under the tree kept you awake many nights. You counted the presents more than a dozen times, and you dreamed a hundred dreams of what might be hiding in those boxes.

Your recollection of the true thrill you once felt may be deadened by your slumber, but if you purposefully retrace your memory, you'll recall those dreams you had. Why is it now so difficult to feel any giddiness at all over the adventure that lies before you?

As you grew older, the childhood dreams of Saturdays and birthdays and Christmas were replaced by lifetime dreams that you were sure would fulfill you. You dreamed of having children who would play happily in the backyard and a spouse who would sit with you on the porch and laugh at their antics.

You dreamed of making enough money to spend countless hours leisurely enjoying a relaxed life, or taking in the wonders of the world on many extended vacations.

You dreamed of a soul mate to cuddle in the mornings while the rich aroma of coffee wafted gently through the room.

Or perhaps your dreams were more ambitious or more adventurous. A significant ministry in which thousands would depend on your brilliant guidance, or a career that would pay large dividends, filled with peers who would stand in awe at your value and skill. A large house handsomely decorated, with a Porsche parked in a three-car garage, maybe two Porsches, or a Porsche and a Hummer. The winning Powerball ticket that would set you finally and completely free to buy a yacht and an island.

These are the common dreams of many.

Whatever your dreams, they were well drawn and they fueled your ambition. They were why you followed the path you eventually took. You went to college because an education was necessary to satisfy your dream of becoming a physician. Or you skipped college to marry the man or the woman who was sure to fulfill other dreams. You leveraged what earthly possessions you owned to purchase your first home or to buy your first car.

At some point, however, you began to suspect that those dreams might not satisfy you as you assumed they would. Although you dreamed of children, you're struggling with infertility, or you have children who fill your days with worry and frustration.

You dreamed of leisure and vacations, but as it turned out, you make barely enough money to pay the bills, much less go on extended trips around the world. There is very little if any leisure time in your life.

The dream of pastoring a church has long since faded or been dashed by the very church you intended to serve. The education required to launch you on that brilliant career as a physician became too expensive to complete, and you settled for far less. In the morning it's body odor, not the aroma of coffee, that awakes you. The Porsche parked in your three-car garage is actually a Corolla parked in a one-car stall.

Or, worse, you *have* fulfilled your dream of becoming a pastor, but have found that pastoring brings more burdens than satisfaction. You do have a brilliant career but can't seem to find any time to enjoy its rewards, and when you do find time, the rewards are far less satisfying than you imagined. You *do* own a Porsche parked in a three-car garage, but it long ago lost its appeal. In fact, you've achieved every dream you once conceived, and they've all fallen short. There is nothing left to dream of. You are in the full throes of a midlife crisis.

If you haven't reached the point where you realize that all the promises of life fail miserably, you will soon enough.

Even a cursory glance at our society reveals the simple fact that most people are not happily living their dreams. If they seem to be, some simple probing reveals otherwise. A recent study of lottery winners well makes the case. Within a mere six months of winning large sums of money, nearly all lottery winners surveyed characterized their lives as no more fulfilled than six months prior to their winning.

Our magazine racks are littered with covers promising more happiness. More satisfaction in sex, more satisfaction in relationships, a better diet to make you feel better about yourself. Why? Because we all want the kind of happiness we don't have. Yet, like the ever-failing diet, the dissatisfaction always returns, and at some point we begin to settle for less happiness than we once dreamed of.

And what about the pleasures of this life? The pleasures that held out great promise when you were an adolescent lose their luster after you've had your fill of them. If we don't see the world clearly, our lives may well become a long string of disappointments punctuated by dwindling pleasures.

This is the human condition. This is the ultimate conclusion of so many philosophies. This is the state of most people, whether Christian or Muslim or Hindu. This is the honest observation of the bumper sticker we all know so well: *Life sucks, and then you die.*

But why? Why is true satisfaction so hard to grasp? And above all, why is genuine happiness so elusive for the Christian, who is supposed to live a fully satisfied life in Christ, brimming with happiness and joy unspeakable?

Unsatisfied Christians

The general failure of life to produce the happiness of achieving dreams is especially interesting for Christians because, judging by their actions rather than their claims, Christians on the whole are no more happy than people of other faiths.

It's the open secret of the church—we make all kinds of incredible claims based on the holy Scriptures, but our lives are pretty much the same as the lives of the unchurched. We live with the same problems and suffer the same challenges. Look at the divorce rate as of September 2004 for an unequivocal benchmark of the lack of satisfaction found among married couples. According to The Barna Group, 35 percent of all

> It's the open secret of the church—we make all kinds of incredible claims based on the holy Scriptures, but our lives are pretty much the same as the lives of the unchurched.

non-born-again couples end their relationship in divorce. And what about born-again couples? The same—35 percent.

Talk to other Christians about the stark similarity between the lives of those who go to church every Sunday and the lives of those who do not. You may get defiance from those who haven't been presented with the statistics, but you'll find the secret isn't as secretive as it used to be. You'll get more and more sighs and nods at suggestions that Christians aren't really so different from non-Christians, certainly not on the scale you would expect considering the promises of love, joy, and peace boldly pronounced from thousands of pulpits across the land. We spend our money on the same kinds of entertainment, we buy the same kinds of foods and clothes, and we spend as much time searching for purpose.

Don't misunderstand me, there are exceptions. There are communities of thriving disciples all over the world who are burning with passion for Christ and filled with joy at their lot in life, pleased to be given yet one more day to sing of their Redeemer's mercy. These are the people who groan inwardly for the day they will meet their Creator face-to-face.

But on the whole, Christianity has failed to satisfactorily respond to the glaring observation that Christians, despite a tendency to describe themselves as happy, are in practice no more happy than non-Christians. Our religion's answer has been predictable: *Seek more, sin less, and have faith. Then you will find happiness in your marriage and on earth.*

Most Christians have followed this mantra in spurts, yet they invariably end up dissatisfied with the results. Their marriages still fail. Their jobs are still downsized. Their cars still break down. Their health still wanes. And they still can't seem to find enough faith to ignore their general predicament in life or embrace the great happiness they once had as naive children.

As a result, Christians settle for less and call it being content in much the same way the world settles for less and calls it being content.

Christianity, it turns out, looks less and less like a child's blissful Christmas, and more and more like a long slide down the hill of hard realities shared by humans in general.

Why?

The answer is quite simple. It begins with a wonderful, revolutionary truth highly esteemed by the early church, but forgotten in our day. That truth is: This life is powerless to satisfy our dreams of great happiness and pleasure. These dreams can be satisfied only in a mind-bending reality that awaits us in the next life. As long as Christians are asleep to this reality, they will search in vain for any lasting fulfillment.

Unfortunately, most Christians *have* fallen asleep to the mind-bending reality that awaits us.

Christianity is in a slumber.

I'm not saying that the religion of Christianity has slipped into slumber. I'm not saying that our *faith* has fallen asleep, necessarily. I'm not speaking about any failure to live good Christian lives. I'm not saying we all are going to hell with FedEx labels plastered on our foreheads.

I'm simply saying that the prevailing teaching of Christianity has become preoccupied with finding true pleasure and happiness and purpose on earth rather than in the age to come. As a result, Christians, who are saved into a faith preoccupied with salvation in the next life, quickly fall asleep to the bliss

> Christianity has become preoccupied with finding true pleasure and happiness and purpose on earth rather than in the age to come.

that awaits them—and their slumber makes the very happiness they seek on earth impossible.

Most Christians are either asleep to the bliss of the afterlife and awake to the pleasures of this life, or asleep to both. We must awaken passion for both, because, as we will see, they are critically dependent on each other.

The pleasures of this life and the happiness they bring have been dealt a death blow by a systemic lack of passion for the next life.

The gravest concern we now face is the fact that our *hope* for the afterlife has slipped into slumber. Our hope for heaven has fallen asleep. And when I say heaven, I mean Christ in heaven, for he is the Light of heaven, of the afterlife, of all the glory that awaits us.

In reading the New Testament, we see the writers repeatedly expressed their insatiable longing for their own inheritance, the hope of glory. For the bliss that awaited them. But the groaning for the afterlife so often expressed by these early writers has become a moan of boredom in the church today. We are more interested in the pleasures of this life than the bliss of the next.

Let me put it plainly: We have here in this life many foretastes of the bliss that awaits us, but unless we know what those foretastes are of, they will never satisfy us. Unless we become desperate for the bliss of the next life, we will never enjoy this life.

The fact is, nothing in this life can satisfy unless it is fully bathed in an obsession for eternity. Nothing. Not a purpose-driven life, not a grand adventure, not the love of a dashing prince or the hand of a beautiful maiden.

Not a thousand hours of leisure time or a hundred exotic vacations.

Not a great marriage or wonderful children or pets that seem to love us dearly.

Not a large boat or an expansive celebrity mansion or a vacation to an island in the Caribbean.

Not success or fame or the popularity we ascribe to those who have either.

Not a large church filled with a thousand worshippers or an expanding ministry to the poor or the healing of a thousand limbs.

Not our religion, our faith, or any version of Christianity less focused on the prize that awaits.

These all will fail our need for unencumbered happiness. We will always be torn and frustrated, no matter how much rejoicing we do this side of death, unless we awaken a new passion for heaven on earth.

The Pleasures of Life

Think of your life as a story. Without the climax of that story, the entire experience is a disappointment.

What happens when the film breaks ten minutes before the end of a movie you've waited months to see? You moan with disappointment! You demand a refund. All that has preceded the missing climax feels empty.

So it is with the stories of our lives. They exist for the climax! We, my friends, were created for climax.

> We have fallen asleep to any tangible hope for the bliss of the afterlife and embraced earthly pleasure as a substitute.

Only when our eyes are fixed on the climax of our faith, which is the next life, can the many pleasures given to us in this life bring satisfaction.

The good pleasures given to us by our Father, and the God-breathed passion we have for discovering that pleasure, were meant to drive us toward the afterlife. Yet we have fallen asleep to any tangible hope for the bliss of the afterlife and embraced earthly pleasure as a substitute.

Even now my mention of *bliss* falls rather flat, doesn't it? Perhaps your mind has been dulled by sleep, and this climax of life doesn't enthrall you as it once did. If you are like most Christians, you are so distracted by the adventures and purpose of this life that what thoughts you do have of the great climax of your faith are ill-defined and thoroughly uninspiring.

Don't misunderstand me—I have no intention of directing you away from the pleasures of this life. To the contrary, I will argue that these incredible gifts we call pleasure are *necessary* for our appreciation of heaven. They are indeed heaven on earth, so to speak, and we were created to seek pleasure. To the extent we can embrace the gifts as intended, we will have a picture of the bliss to come that will inflame our passion for eternity.

We must relieve pleasure of the false expectation we've placed on it to fully satisfy. We must see pleasure as simply a foretaste—only then can we be left panting for a far greater bliss.

Once you embrace this new understanding, your bread will taste sweeter. Succulent meats will ravage your taste buds; music will sweep you away; sunsets will numb your mind; love will fill you with warm longing. Pleasure will come alive in a way you never imagined.

Yet, stripped of a preoccupation with heaven, this life and all its pleasures will continue to disappoint you, because life isn't really about purpose or adventure in your allotted time on earth. It's more about the purpose and adventure of eternity. You will find great happiness for this life only when you lose yourself to the climax of the next life.

Short of that climax, there is no true satisfaction, even for Christians.

Satisfaction comes hard when the eyes of your heart are closed

> When the eyes of your heart are opened to the staggering experience that awaits you, the gates that hold back lasting satisfaction in your life will be blown off their hinges.

to the prize at the end of the race. But when the eyes of your heart are opened to the staggering experience that awaits you, the gates that hold back lasting satisfaction in your life will be blown off their hinges.

Then you, along with Paul, will groan for that day of bliss.

Then you will wait in eager anticipation for a fast-approaching day, like a bride who waits for her wedding; like a child waiting for Christmas. Then your life will be filled with a new and living hope that will consume you with delight now, while you wait. Then a bright light of hope will shine back on this life from eternity and illuminate the pleasures around you.

This hope in no way minimizes the work of Christ on the cross to deliver us from the bondage of sin now, while we run the race. But we will experience our final escape from sin only in that final day of ecstasy. In the meantime, our access to that day of bliss is found through the pleasures of God and in particular through a portal called *hope*.

It is critical that we begin to understand our great slumber and awaken to reclaim our incredible and enviable inheritance. It is time we begin to hope, *really* hope, for the incomparable riches that await us.

It is time we begin to feast once again, now on the foretastes of heaven, and with a new appreciation for what those tastes precede.

It is time we stop being *driven* from a world of disappointments and start being *drawn* by the light of glory, like moths to flame.

The world's bumper sticker reads: *Life sucks, and then you die.*

Perhaps Christian bumper stickers should read: *Life sucks, but then you find hope and you can't wait to die.*

One of my favorite quotes from C. S. Lewis is found in his book *The Weight of Glory*. Listen:

> Indeed if we consider the unblushing promises of reward and the staggering nature of the rewards promised in the gospels, it would seem that our Lord finds our desires not too strong, but too weak. We are halfhearted creatures, fooling about with drink and sex and ambition when infinite joy is offered to us, like an ignorant child who wants to go on making mud pies in the slum because he cannot imagine what is meant by the offer of a holiday by the sea. We are far too easily pleased.

I have no intention of minimizing the pleasures God has given us here on earth, as I see them as critical to embracing the hope of greater such pleasures to come. Yet, like Lewis, I agree that the church's passion is anywhere but on the holiday by the sea.

If you follow with me on this journey of discovery, I will help you see your own slumber. If you continue that journey to the end, you'll hopefully be awakened from that slumber.

Your fundamental view of life and faith will be challenged and changed. Then, and only then, will you be able to look at the adventure set before you on this earth and embrace it with the kind of anticipation a child has for Christmas.

Our journey will consist of two primary legs. The remaining chapters in Part I will examine the slumber we have fallen into and explain how we were lulled into sleep. The four chapters of Part II will concern themselves with how we can awaken from that slumber.

Hold on tight, my friends.

2

The Search for Pleasure

One Man's Journey to Discover Happiness (Part One)

I've made some strong claims about Christianity's failure to awaken a passion for true happiness in most believers' lives. In the chapters that follow, I will explain and support these claims, but I want to begin examining our search for happiness and our descent into slumber by looking at one man's story.

My story. My own quest to understand King Solomon's claim that there is nothing better to do in this life than find happiness and satisfaction (Eccl. 3:12). My own quest for bliss and subsequent descent into a slumber that deadened my life for many years. Perhaps if we examine my slumber, we can better understand the nature of this odd condition that has lulled so many Christians into darkness.

I've chosen my story because I know it well, not because it's any more interesting or provocative than yours. Because we all are the same in so many ways. I am certain that you will see yourself in this story of discovery.

My Quest for Bliss

Imagine looking into a glass bubble. Inside you see a miniature city with a beautiful church and a little girl on ice skates. When you shake it, tiny white flecks swirl around like snow. Now pretend that this bubble represents an entire culture. Could be a Chinese bubble or an American bubble. Could even be one called the church. Whatever the case, the bubble is your world.

My particular bubble was formed in an exotic land far away. The advent of cross-cultural missions spawned a unique breed of Christians who left one bubble to take their message of liberation into another bubble. Every few years they would return to the home bubble to recharge their batteries and reestablish their identities before striking back out to the foreign bubble. But in the process they bore children who had no real connection to the bubble their parents grew up in, and found themselves outsiders in the foreign bubble. They were stranded outside both bubbles.

My father, John Dekker, is a Dutchman from Holland, and my mother, Helen, is an American from Montana. They became Canadians for ease of travel, boarded a ship, and left the North American bubble for a bubble known as Indonesia. There I was born, a Dutch/American/Canadian/Indonesian, in a bubble trapped within the Stone Age.

One of the clearest memories I have from those early years is of a six-year-old child standing outside a concrete building with bars on the windows to keep the thieves out. Tears stream silently down the boy's cheeks. He's staring up at a lighted door through which a nine-year-old girl, his sister, peers out. Night has fallen, and a sticky tropical stillness has settled over the boarding school compound. A steady chorus of insect sounds emanates from the nearby jungle.

The boy has worked up the courage to sneak out of his dormitory because he's worried that he might be dying. It's his chest, you see. He's been crying all day, and he thinks that his heart might stop. He knows that his parents love him, but they are far away doing God's work in the jungle. The dormitory parents probably love him, too, but there are a hundred other kids, and they aren't sure how to show any of them love.

The boy asks his sister if he can talk to her. But she can't risk breaking the rules. Her eyes tear up, and she tells the boy that he has to go away from her window before he gets into trouble.

He turns and shuffles slowly back to bed. Now he's quite sure his heart will indeed stop.

The boy is me, and I've just learned that I am alone. I don't fit. I am a boy who has no home, no culture, no real family, and no friends who have any of the above. I must create my own little bubble where I can live, safe and secure.

> I can't say that my particular kind of not-belonging was any different from yours, or from millions of others'—it was just more pervasive than most. So began my lifelong quest to discover happiness.

I can't say that my particular kind of not-belonging was any different from yours, or from millions of others'—it was just more pervasive than most. So began my lifelong quest to discover happiness. Later I would characterize that quest with three questions:

1. *Who am I?*

2. *Where do I belong?*

3. *Am I happy?*

There is a children's book called *Are You My Mother?* about a lost bird who goes from animal to animal seeking his mother. When I think of my childhood, I think of that book.

Searching for a Home

Like any child born into this world of wonder, my nights of loneliness were tempered by the delights to be discovered on every side: BB guns and forging rapids and smoking out bees for golden honey. Swimming in the crashing ocean waves next to old rusted tanks left by the American army after World War II. Trekking up mountains to discover waterfalls, hacking through the jungle in search of fighter planes shot down in the last war.

I was married at age seven. Yes, it was a bit early, but Theresa Mungello was just too cute to wait on, and I was desperate to belong to someone. There was a great deal of planning, and we performed the ceremony with white flowers, using a cardboard box as a pulpit. It was the highlight of my year, bar none. It brought me some happiness.

My parents were devastated by the prevailing practice of sending their children away to a boarding school at such a young age, but without any reasonable alternative, they complied. My sister and I wrote letters home once a week, and our parents visited for a weekend once every semester.

I remember being sick with pneumonia once. The nurse made me cough into a bowl while hitting my back to loosen the phlegm. My mother came out for the weekend and sat by my bed. When you're sick you get lots of love—this is a good thing.

But then Sunday night came, and my mother had to take the plane home early the next morning. She was leaving me! I was lying in bed with a high fever, coughing up phlegm, delirious with anguish over the prospect of her leaving, but none of this mattered. She was crying and I was crying, but she was still leaving.

Who am I? Where do I belong? Am I happy?

Like many others, I can recall a string of definitive moments including standing among a group of perhaps a dozen children while two captains chose teams for soccer or basketball. I was actually quite athletic but not as skilled as the other children who escaped into sports. Hearing the other names called off one by one without mine being among them was a kind of free fall into the bottomless hole of worthlessness. I didn't care, of course. Or so I let on. I would pretend to talk to someone else who hadn't been picked yet about the math test that morning. I would elevate myself above the pitiful state of giving two hoots what anyone thought.

But like all who are subjected to such declarations of value-lessness, my heart would grow sicker with each name called. When I was one of the last two picked, I knew that I was worthless. I did not belong with these boys, and I desperately hoped that none of the girls had seen.

The incident with the pneumonia must have struck a chord in me, because when I was in the sixth grade, I came up with a plan to use illness to my advantage. The ingenuity of the human spirit hard at work.

I convinced a friend of mine named Guy that sick people were especially loved. They were cared for and nurtured. After much talk, we decided to go to the clinic and declare that we were feeling ill.

The nurse, a loving woman whom I will always admire, named Beth Rainey, took our temperatures and noted no elevation, but she let us rest for a few hours in the sickroom near the clinic where ill children remained under her care.

She quickly concluded that our bright smiles and bantering in the sickroom weren't consistent with illness, so she declared us better and sent us off, much to our dismay.

After a few days, Guy and I became lonely for the sickroom again. Being under the watchful care of the nurse was a dream worth pursuing. We decided that if we were to demonstrate our feigned illnesses by vomiting, we would certainly be admitted and cared for. And if throwing up wasn't enough, we could fill our mouths with hot water the moment before entering the sickroom so the thermometer would read high.

For several days we practiced vomiting by sticking our fingers down our throats until we gagged something up. Truly, we were committed to our quest for the nurse's care.

The plan worked perfectly, and we were once again admitted to the sickroom. But once again, Beth Rainey proved that a schooling in medicine had rewarded her with an above-average understanding of illness. And once again, unable to reproduce the smell of vomit on our breath as we had earlier and elevate our temperatures under her watchful eye, we were declared recovered and sent back to the dormitory.

I became desperate to be ill. I wanted to be cared for. If only

I really could be sick and tended to every few hours. The notion of such care was too much for me to ignore at this point in my life. I decided I must become ill.

My plan of eating rotten fruit until I was truly and hopelessly sick was too much for Guy. But he did swear to silence. And so I began to eat rotten fruit.

And I became sick.

I was admitted into the sickroom on a Saturday. Wiser than before, I timed the nurse's routine and drank hot water before her rounds. I spent Saturday night in the warm comfort of illness's embrace.

But there was a problem. I was alone in the room. Apart from the nurse's visits, I was in total isolation. By Sunday afternoon I had become quite lonely. I will never forget Sunday evening. It was a quiet night, desperately quiet. The cicadas screamed softly in the nearby jungle. And at about seven o'clock a song drifted through the windows.

The other children and roughly a hundred missionaries who'd gathered for Sunday evening services were all singing "How Great Thou Art." But all I could hear was "How Small You Are"—me, not God. The isolation of the sickroom swallowed me, and a terrible loneliness set in. I was abandoned. After going to such lengths to belong somewhere, I was learning that somewhere was really nowhere.

Who am I? Where do I belong? Am I happy?

I began to cry. And as on the night my mother left me with pneumonia, I could not stop for a long time. No one could even hear me.

Spreading My Wings

By the time I entered the seventh grade, I had learned who I was. I was inside more than I was outside; that is, I lived inside myself, in dreams and fantasies, more than I lived in my immediate surroundings.

My God-given search for happiness had already led me to the suspicion that the world was unfair. That I couldn't depend on others to care for me. That I couldn't really trust myself to care for me. What I had was the great assurance that true meaning and happiness existed either somewhere beyond what I could see or inside my own mind. My fledgling faith had not delivered on the promise to deliver me from a lonely world. Still, I had my dreams.

On the outside I might be the last one picked for soccer, but in my dreams I was a superstar who scored goals in the most spectacular fashion. Bicycle kicks were a thing of ease for me. Double and triple bicycle kicks that had the fans roaring with approval. I could weave between defenders with super-human ease.

On the outside I might not be a hero, but on the inside I was a protector of all that was good and holy.

My happiest days were spent at home in the jungle on vacation. I would wake early, throw on a pair of shorts, and head out to the forest. Such trivial coverings like shirts and shoes were for the weak. I was a kid born of the jungle, for the jungle. This was my domain, and I would dominate it.

The natives could perform spectacular feats, racing down muddy, rooted footpaths with hardly a slip, shimmying up trees with the ease of walking. I was determined to match them in every way.

I remember walking through the jungle with my brother, Danny, arguing endlessly about whether American shoes could outperform bare feet on a muddy slope. He was only two years younger than me and without question my closest friend, so it was with a certain horror that I denounced his insistence that shoes were better than bare feet. How could my brother, of all people, betray me with such an outlandish notion? I would prove him wrong.

And I did. Many times.

I relished comics, in particular *Spider-Man* and *Daredevil*.

The prospect of whipping up into the trees and slinging from branch to branch with the ease shown by Daredevil as he crossed city rooftops awed me. For hours on end I would walk beneath the canopy and dream of flying through the trees to defeat evil. This was no casual boyhood distraction—it was an obsession. A drive to discover meaning and happiness beyond the here and now.

Although my native friends didn't make a practice of swinging from tree to tree, I convinced them that they should. We practiced endlessly, counting the number of trees we could traverse without touching the ground.

It was there in the jungle that I first unleashed my imagination, spread my wings and soared with eagles that winked at the trouble beneath them. In my mind, I was someone special, a superhero. I had been ostracized by a world that didn't truly understand who I was, but alone in the jungle I was a force to be reckoned with. Nothing could stop me; no one could abandon me. I was home.

Unfortunately, the disappointing reality of life invariably found a way to crush the liberation I had crafted for myself. Trees planted in the ground were always much harder to navigate than those growing in my mind. The whips tethered to my waist would rarely strike their intended villains as I'd imagined. The panty hose I pulled over my head did no great justice to the masks in the pictures. And the villains were never real bad guys with bad names.

Love, the Forbidden Fruit

When I was in the ninth grade, I crossed the ocean and attended a boarding high school in Papua New Guinea. I did two things in high school: I rode dirt bikes and I fell in love. Motorcycles and girls—these were my newest obsessions. Each had their own ways of elevating me out of the mundane.

As I look back now, I see with complete clarity that the path of my life followed a long and determined quest for happiness, although I didn't recognize it as such until I was well into my thirties. I longed for happiness. For security and nurturing and love and passion. My hopes were in reaching beyond myself to embrace a reality much larger than what I could see around me. I wanted to touch the sky and fly through the trees and save the world. I wanted to come face-to-face with God, and I wanted to love and be loved by the girls.

Having survived the annulment of my marriage to Theresa Mungello, whom I wed in the second grade, my next great love was a teenage girl named Lee Ann Eby. I had just arrived at the high school far from the jungles I'd grown up in, and the first thing I noticed was that all the older boys wanted to date this particularly spunky girl named Lee Ann. I couldn't blame them—she exuded confidence and beauty and a kind of seductive charm that made me go to great lengths in considering how I might secure her friendship.

Daredevil may have simply walked past her in his red suit, made eye contact, and nodded, thereby immediately capturing her heart. I was neither so bold nor red suited, so I worked up the courage to have a friend pass her a note suggesting that she date boys her age. Boys like me. To my surprise, she agreed.

I remember the first time I held Lee Ann's hand walking down a dark alley. It began with one of those brush once, brush twice contacts that send electricity through your heart. We walked hand in hand on the hard gravel road, but I was walking on the clouds. We were soul mates. And when she abandoned me later that year to once again answer the call of an older boy, I sobbed uncontrollably. That night stands out in my memory as one of my worst. I stood in the dark behind one of the school buildings, crying, and I remember wondering why I couldn't stop. The anguish swept over me in terrible, unrelenting waves.

My family returned to America for a one-year furlough when I was in the tenth grade, and it was there I first tasted the forbidden fruit of love. A kiss.

I don't remember the name of the first girl I kissed, but she was short, with cropped blonde hair and blue eyes, and I fell hopelessly in love with her the first week I attended the private school in west Chicago. I suppose she was enamored with the new jungle boy, because after a day or two we somehow ended up walking together hand in hand. I had done this before, and I was energized with self-confidence.

Determined to impress her, I told mind-bending stories of eating spiders and racing through the jungle barefoot, and I filled the stories with as many exotic details as I could shoehorn into the truth.

And it worked.

I'll never forget the moment. We were sitting on the steps that led to the chapel when she suddenly looked up at me with those dove eyes and asked if she could kiss me.

Imagine that! She was asking me! And to the best of my recollection, the look on her face was one of total adoration. My heart was beating like a tom drum. I swallowed, desperate to hide the sudden terror that had immobilized me.

> She leaned forward and pressed her lips to mine. Immediately my head swam. She held the kiss for a long time, wet and crazy and terribly intoxicating.
>
> No man can come face-to-face with heaven and return to normal life without weak bones.

"Yes," I croaked.

She leaned forward and pressed her lips to mine. Immediately my head swam. She held the kiss for a long time, wet and crazy and terribly intoxicating. When she stood, I tried to stand with her, but I couldn't find the strength. I had just tasted heaven, after all, and no man can come face-to-face with heaven and return to normal life without weak bones. Oh, what a foretaste of glory divine.

I remember nothing else from that day. My memory was permanently blinded by the bright light of that first kiss. This was the truest, most relevant, most satisfying kind of happiness, there could be no doubt.

And then I saw her giggling with an upperclassman several days later, and I became numb. Horror. Surely she hadn't abandoned me for this thug already!

But there she sat, staring into his eyes. I knew that stare. I had been swept away by it myself. For days I lived in a kind of stupor. It was because I wasn't American enough, I decided. I had to become like the other kids. I had to dump the foolish jungle boy nonsense and become a true red-blooded American. Then I could and would recover the happiness I had discovered on the chapel steps.

This was 1979, and disco was in its prime. There was a homecoming dance coming up. If I could just learn to move on the floor like John Travolta and wow my love with spins and dips, she would toss aside the other toad and leap into my arms.

I purchased a book that promised to teach me the finest moves, retreated to my upstairs bedroom, slipped in an Earth Wind & Fire cassette, and followed the steps on the page. For hours over many days I practiced. Each day at school I kept my eyes on my love and the upperclassman thug, knowing a secret that neither of them could possibly know: their silly little love romp was about to crash and burn.

When the book called for a partner, I commandeered the reluctant help of my younger brother, Danny. Together we danced, hand in hand, arm in arm, stumbling over each other's feet until my brother fell to the floor, laughing hysterically.

I did not laugh. This was serious business. My love was at stake. I was becoming a man who could walk on the clouds with a goddess, and silliness was no way to embrace such heady objectives. I demanded his silence and his cooperation. Over time I learned to fling my flares about the creaking floorboards fairly well, I thought.

Then the big night came. My girl was there with the toad. I stared across the room in silence as they gazed into each other's eyes in a rapture that immediately crushed my elaborate fantasy of splitting the room with my sleek moves. In fact, while watching them dance it occurred to me that their steps were superior to mine. I never even attempted to talk to her.

I crawled home at midnight feeling utterly foolish. But this time I did not sob or cry or even shed one tear. I was beyond that. My shell was hardening. I would just have to find another way past the skin of this mundane world into the bliss that beckoned.

I look back on 1979 as a year of distinguished failure. I was very unhappy.

Who am I? Where do I belong? Am I happy?

But not all was lost. Back in the familiar world of the jungle, I cast an entirely different light on my yearlong hiatus. I had traveled to the exotic world of America as a boy and returned to New Guinea as a man bearing many fresh insights and talents. Once again I became the hero. A Tarzan calling to his Jane. Once again I won the admiration of my first true love, Lee Ann Eby.

I would like to say that I taught her how to kiss beside the bamboo shoots one cool fall evening, but I am sure she'd been kissed before. By an older boy, undoubtedly. Still, none of their kisses could possibly have filled her with such passion as mine. After all, I had learned from a girl who'd fallen head-over-heels for me in America.

At least, that was my version.

Embracing the World

As the son of missionaries, I grew up as a Christian. And I approached my pursuit of God with the same energy I had expended on my other quests for happiness. If there was a God to be found, I was going to find him. And there was a God, naturally, so I did find him.

But I did not find precisely what I was looking for. I did not find a warrior in a chariot, sweeping down from the sky to deliver me from my loneliness. When I spoke to the mountains, they did not move. When I screamed at them with a terrible determination, they did not even waver. When I demanded that he deliver the love of a particular passionate kisser in Chicago in 1979, either God did not see fit to grant my request or the girl was in rebellion.

I expressed my zeal for my parents' religion by street witnessing and preaching on the occasions when I convinced the leaders to give me the pulpit for an evening. I remember entering the home of some Muslims with two friends and boldly proclaiming the gospel when I was in the eighth grade. I became so passionate in my presentation that I felt I had to do something radical, so I mounted the kitchen table, stood to my full height, and leveled the truth with conviction.

I forget which of my friends started laughing first, but my behavior suddenly struck me as preposterous. We all were soon in tears with laughter.

Who am I? Where do I belong? Am I happy?

When I came to the United States to attend college, I severed all ties to my past, determined to find happiness in a world that had dealt me numerous cruel blows. I was eager to discover the full measure of life that had eluded me thus far. My quest for happiness had given me some understanding, but I concluded that on balance my search had failed to deliver what I was looking for: true happiness. The happiness I found was always fleeting. Abandoning me at every turn.

At first my turn from Christianity was a gentle, private affair. No one knew my doubts. No one suspected my profound disappointment with Christianity. I knew the game well enough to play my cards expertly, and I had the confidence to persuade all those who watched that I was winning. But there would quickly come a point when that turn from Christianity would be too severe to hide.

During my first year of college I embraced American culture with open arms. Wine, women, and song!

Actually, not as much wine as I would have liked—the

Christian university I was attending frowned on drunkenness. And the women—well, let's just say that my numerous attempts at understanding, much less winning, American women turned out quite miserably. I just couldn't get my groove down. I had no problem getting girls to talk to me, but the moment I began spilling my most eloquent philosophies of life, they turned a deaf ear. Or worse, smirked.

I decided that this side of the world was even more cruel than I had estimated.

Then I had the occasion to spend a week with my first true love, Lee Ann, during the summer break. Flames of passion were once again lit. We were soul mates from a distant land, and we immediately embraced the fact that other Americans could no more fulfill our needs and desires than a sparrow could try to find happiness with a turkey.

So it happened that in my sophomore year, I asked Lee Ann, who then lived in Nashville, to marry me. One year later we were married.

Finally, I was well suited to continue my journey of discovery, I thought. There was a profound world of meaning out there, brimming with fulfillment and happiness and all the things that we humans spend our lives searching for, and I was determined to find it. To assist in my own search, I switched my major to religious studies and my minor to philosophy and applied to attend Evangel University in Springfield, Missouri.

Lee Ann and I were in the first year of our marriage, living in a roach-infested ten-by-thirty trailer on campus, and happiness was in full swing. It was there, studying philosophy and religion and creative writing, that I first discovered the power of words. I remember sitting in front of a computer, watching the words I typed appear magically before me on the amber screen. I wrote poems and papers and developed an insatiable appetite for more. More knowledge, more words. I lost myself to discovering the truth of all that was.

And I was well on my way when I awoke alone in bed one

morning to a horrifying thought unveiled by several months of intense philosophical investigations.

God doesn't exist.

I sat up in bed, wide-eyed. *What was that?*

God might not exist.

Please, be quiet already and get some sleep.

But I couldn't sleep. What if it was true? What if everything in which I thus far had rooted my own discovery of meaning turned out to be false?

> What if it was true? What if everything in which I thus far had rooted my own discovery of meaning turned out to be false?

For several days I tried my best to ignore my suspicion of God's nonexistence, but the more I did so, the more compelling the suspicion seemed. I couldn't hide this terrible hunch any longer.

Imagine my young wife's eyes when I sat her down and announced my newfound revelation: *God does not exist.* At the very least, we can't know that he exists, which is just as bad.

Eventually, Lee Ann took it all in stride. She knew me as the thinker who had frequently led groups in exercises of contemplation. I had given myself to endless hours of philosophical debate from the first day she'd met me. I had always been voracious in my need for understanding. This was simply another exercise. I would surely snap out of it soon enough, and we could get back to being good Christians, equally yoked.

But the exercise didn't end that week. Or the next. Or the next year. A considerable amount of time would pass before I rediscovered the faith I once knew as a child. These years were without doubt the most miserable of my life. I tried desperately to believe, but I could not. I beat at my brain against evidence that demanded a verdict, but invariably found no verdict at all.

I was willing to try anything besides intellectual suicide, because I reasoned that if there was a God who created me, he would reveal himself to me in a way that was absolutely consistent with my intellect, assuming my intellect, not only my body, was a part of his creation.

We graduated from Evangel University and headed for California to embrace real life. Finally, real, real life. High school behind, college degree in hand, soul mate at side. Time to take on the world for real. Time to find real happiness.

Was I a Christian?

Who am I? Where do I belong? Am I happy?

By a thin sliver of stubborn faith, I clung to the barest belief that I was a new creature, transformed by a power that resided in and through Christ. I had boldly proclaimed my faith on hundreds of occasions. I had been filled with his Spirit. I was the son of missionaries. Surely I was a Christian. Surely I was saved. I was certainly as Christian and as saved as 99 percent of all the faithfully churched I knew who called themselves Christians.

But was I a *disciple* of Christ? Was I following Jesus? No, not really. Not hardly at all. Amazingly, few of even my closest friends recognized this fact.

I was, after all, a Christian.

There I was, the product of twenty-some-odd years of searching for happiness, and I hadn't yet found it. At least none that lasted more than a short time. Everyone thought of me as a happy person, I think. But deep down, where none of them could see, I was lost.

I was trying to embrace real life, but in real life I was near the bottom.

3

Foundations

The Heart of the Matter

By now you're seeing a pattern in my life that's similar to the search we all undertake in this life. Before I conclude the story of my journey, we must examine some basic issues at work within the story.

Hope, the Emotion That Motivates

Thinking back to my search for happiness in the jungles of Indonesia, I now see that I was simply following the instincts placed in me by God. As a child and through my adolescent years, I navigated my way through life using my basic emotions as a compass. I wanted to belong, to be happy, to feel needed, to feel nurtured. Don't we all?

Unfortunately, happiness, as a raw emotion, has been disparaged in many religious circles today. Many well-meaning people no longer seek happiness at all, but I say it's inhuman not to. We were created for happiness, and whether we admit it or not, we are governed by it.

King Solomon had this to say on the matter:

I know that there is nothing better for men than to be happy and do good while they live. That everyone may eat and drink, and find satisfaction in all his toil—this is the gift of God. (Eccl. 3:12–13)

However else we may characterize God's gifts to us, they all boil down to some form of satisfaction and happiness, Solomon suggested. There is nothing better for us than to be happy and do good while we live.

A simple examination of mankind reveals that we humans spend most of our time doing things that we believe will either immediately or ultimately give us happiness.

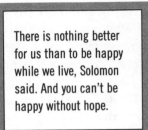

There is nothing better for us than to be happy while we live, Solomon said. And you can't be happy without hope.

This is why we go to school and brush our teeth and get married and look for better jobs. It's why we have children and buy cars and spend large amounts of money on foods that please our palates instead of just shoving the necessary nutrients down our gullets.

These pleasures, as I will call them, do give us a measure of happiness. They are God's gift to enjoy now, for a very specific reason. We were created to search and find these pleasures suggested by Solomon.

I began to question my own happiness early, and I soon discovered that all my friends were asking the same questions. We all wanted to know—the whole world wanted to know—what makes us happy?

For many, the question may change over time from a simple *What makes me happy?* to more specific questions about particular failures in life.

Why do so many of my relationships struggle?

Why do I feel worse about my body with each passing year?

Why is my job so empty?

Why am I such a failure?

A Christian might frame the questions differently: Why is Christianity so boring?

Why do I struggle with my marriage and other relationships if I've been filled with the Spirit and empowered to enjoy his fruits—love, joy, and peace?

Why is true happiness always a moving target, if I already have everything I need in Christ?

Clearly these questions have been asked for as long as humans

> Why is Christianity so boring?
>
> Why do I struggle with my marriage and other relationships if I've been filled with the Spirit and empowered to enjoy his fruits—love, joy, and peace?

have had minds. But in light of the incredible lethargy that is now sweeping through Christendom, the questions must be asked again.

Give Me an Answer

The answer to the most fundamental question—What makes us happy and what makes us sad?—begins with a fresh understanding of precisely what motivates those created in God's image. Happiness is an emotion, and emotion has a profound effect on nearly every critical decision we make. For the moment, let's dispense with the "fact" versus "feeling" talk, which dismisses emotion as a by-product of the Fall, and look straight into the heart of this wonderful gift granted us by God. Let's rephrase the question: what makes us happy and what makes us sad? this way:

What elevates our emotions, and what dashes them to the ground? What makes us jump for joy, and what sends us into a pit of deep discouragement?

The answers are surprisingly simple: Hope. And hopelessness.

If you think about what elevates your mood, you will always

find hope. If you think about what changes your mood from one of happiness to one of sadness, you will always find hope-lessness.

Consider: At one moment you are applying the Right Guard, hurrying around the bedroom in anticipation of a date with Samantha. Your mind is spinning with images of her, and you are full of hope.

The next moment the phone rings. It's Samantha. Something, which she doesn't elaborate on, has come up. She can't go. Your *hopes* are dashed, and you feel crestfallen.

Consider: You're feeling unappreciated and distant from the other women in the church. Your husband has spent an inordinate amount of time at work lately and hasn't taken time for you. You're left alone at home to slave over the stove. Life is not a bowl of cherries.

Then the phone rings. It's Linda. She and some of the other ladies are going out for a movie night and want you to come. You hang up the phone, buoyed by a fresh sense of purpose and meaning. Something as simple and as insignificant as the *hope* of a night out with the girls has changed your day.

Hope and hopelessness impact our sense of well-being, even when we encounter them in tiny portions. Encouragement and discouragement, a sense of success or failure, our drive to get out of bed in the morning—all are guided by hope or hopelessness.

In fact, we would be best served by recognizing that every hour of life is lived somewhere between hope and hopelessness.

Hope is the primary force that drives human beings from hour to hour. Hope for a simple pleasure, a hug, a kiss, a juicy rib eye cooked to perfection. A new red Corvette, a beautiful home, a long vacation in Europe. The renewed health of an ill child or aging mother. These are among the many hopes that motivate our daily lives. Everything we do is driven by hope or hopelessness in one form or another.

Seeing Life Through the Lens of Hope

Hear me clearly. It is critical that we accept the notion that our search for happiness is what primarily steers our lives, regardless of what other dogma is delivered from the pulpit.

And it is most critical that we begin to see our *hope* as the single most influential element in achieving happiness. There are other elements that affect our happiness—what is happening in the present moment, for example. But the present is fleeting in a way the future is not, and so it doesn't hold the same power as hope for the future.

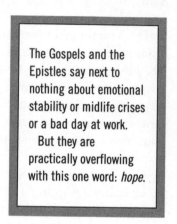

The Gospels and the Epistles say next to nothing about emotional stability or midlife crises or a bad day at work.

But they are practically overflowing with this one word: *hope.*

We must begin looking at our lives through the lens of hope, particularly as people of faith. The Gospels and the Epistles say next to nothing about emotional stability or midlife crises or a bad day at work.

But they are practically overflowing with this one word: *hope.*

A Path of Hopelessness

If there is one universal symptom of hopelessness or depression, it is sleep. *A slumber* could easily be defined as a separation from reality that provides sweet, sweet relief from hopelessness. Think of sleep as a drug that anesthetizes the hopelessness and deadens the pain of life.

We've all seen the movies and heard the groans of those who have lost their motivation to get out of bed. We have all lain awake on the occasional morning, digging deeply for a good reason to roll out of bed and face the hopelessness of the day.

Without exception, hopelessness will call its host to slumber. I might have called this book *The Hopelessness of Christianity* because, as we will see, hopelessness is the reason for the slumber of Christianity.

Again, hear me clearly: The religion called Christianity has lulled millions into a slumber that anesthetizes them from the utter failure of that very Christianity to fulfill the promises so boldly announced upon entry into its ranks.

Surely you remember the call from the pulpit: *Follow me, for my burden is light. Kneel here at this altar, give your life over to Jesus, follow the way of the church, and your life will be miraculously transformed into one abounding with peace and joy. With health and wealth and a thousand benefits that aren't available unless you do kneel and pray.*

You'll have a happy, happy house with a snappy, snappy spouse.

Don't misunderstand me, many of these rewards are indeed promised. But for reasons we will explore later, most Christians never truly experience the lasting rewards of bliss promised by the preacher on that day of entry.

Consider the following casual discussion between two students at Princeton University:

"What are the first few thoughts that drift through your mind when you hear the word *Christian*?" Bill asked. "Besides *church*. Or *boring*."

"Boring?" Susan returned. "I don't know what church you go to, but I don't understand how you can say boring."

"Is that right? Tell me, what's not boring about church?"

"Well . . ." Susan scrambled for words to appropriately communicate just how attractive Christianity could be. She cleared her throat.

"Well, there's fellowship." She quickly corrected her language. "Friendship . . . lots of friends—"

"Are you bored with God?" Bill interrupted.

The question hit Susan broadside. *Bored with God?* "No, of course not."

"No? Then what about God or Jesus excites you?"

"I'm not sure I would characterize him in those terms. He's not a toy you get excited over. God and Christianity are more about abundant life and eternity."

The corners of Bill's mouth edged up in a restrained grin. "Life abundant and eternity. And what exactly are those?"

"Don't patronize me."

He lifted his hand and made a show of wiping the smile from his mouth. "In all seriousness, then. Speak out. Illuminate for me this ecstasy called Christianity."

She started to answer but stopped short, vacant of any reasonable answer. "It's about a relationship," she finally said, trying desperately to piece her reasoning together.

"Relationship? With what, an ideology? 'I love Christ'? Please. What happened to eternity?" Bill sighed. "Face it, Susan. Christianity has become so totally passé. It's an old, stale religion that promises unreasonable, surreal bliss and delivers absolutely nothing immediately tangible. Boring."

"Not true," Susan said. "It delivers plenty that's immediately tangible. And who said bliss is the point, anyway?"

Enough. There's more, but you've heard what you need to hear. Enough to have peered through a window into the greatest challenge facing Christ's followers today.

Although Susan certainly has no clue about her predicament, she is fast slipping into a slumber. By entertaining the very thought that life may not be about bliss after all, she is entering a dark room. This is where the slumber begins. Failing to sustain any sort of lasting happiness in her faith, she has begun to dismiss the promise of that happiness as less than critical to her faith.

It's a path we've all taken, and, I assure you, it leads down into a valley, certainly not to the mountaintop. Unless someone shines a bright light of hope into this dark valley, Susan may very well slip into a deep and terrible boredom of eternity, which we are calling the slumber of Christianity.

It will soon affect not only her view of the next life, but her satisfaction in this life.

You're Not in a Slumber? Think Again

Some of you still wonder what on earth I'm speaking about with all this talk of slumber. You've read about Susan's paltry predicament, and you see no reason to wave a red flag of alarm. You're not convinced Susan is even in a prison, visible walls or not. You don't know what all the fuss is about, and I don't blame you. After all, how many times have I felt the same way?

But let me probe with a few less-blunt questions, just to be sure we're on the same page.

How many hours do you spend in prayer before boredom takes over? Or should I say minutes? Perhaps seconds?

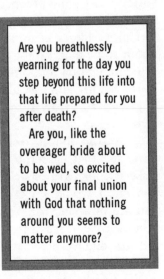

Are you breathlessly yearning for the day you step beyond this life into that life prepared for you after death?

Are you, like the overeager bride about to be wed, so excited about your final union with God that nothing around you seems to matter anymore?

Are you breathlessly yearning for the day you step beyond this life into that life prepared for you after death? Does the hope you have for heaven raise the hair on the back of your neck or make your belly float? Are you obsessed with eternity? Does it preoccupy you, so that all the gifts on this earth pale by comparison?

Are you, like the overeager bride about to be wed, so excited about your final union with God that nothing around you seems to matter anymore?

Do you regularly, as did the apostle Paul, honestly crave to die and be with Christ, because departing to be with him is better *by far* than living to serve him?

These are interesting questions that set the mind in new directions. Perhaps you are slightly more bored with the goal of your faith than you assumed. For that matter, perhaps the great climax of Christianity isn't even an integral part of your faith. Perhaps you were saved into a kind of Christianity entirely different from a faith groaning for the great liberation after death, which was Paul's Christianity.

A few more direct questions: If you once groaned for the day of your redemption, have you lost the unspeakable joy and passion you once felt?

As a Christian, do you feel like the ugly stepchild in this society? Does the prospect of being loudly identified as a follower of Jesus while you wait in the checkout line make you feel more like a criminal about to be arrested than a bride about to be married?

I could go on and on—surely if I broaden my aim I would eventually send an arrow through your heart.

If you no longer feel or have never felt that desperate desire to feast at your Creator's table when you die, I would say it's because you are in a slumber. Your life is bound to be frustrated. Great pleasure and happiness will always evade you.

> You're not alone. From the moment many Christians are first awakened into the kingdom of God's great delights, they begin a slow yet methodical retreat into hopelessness.

Your walk along the path of life will become increasingly hopeless.

And you're not alone. From the moment many Christians are first awakened into the kingdom of God's great delights, they begin a slow yet methodical retreat into hopelessness.

As an author I often have the opportunity to gauge audiences' reactions to probing questions. The one question that produces the most consistent response is similar to the question framed by Bill earlier in this chapter.

"Are you desperately longing for heaven?" I ask.

Invariably I receive a blank stare. *Desperately longing? Heaven?*

I'm going to heaven, the blank stares tell me. *I am looking forward to being with my Father in a place of no sorrows.*

"Yes, but are you obsessed with the bliss awaiting you?"

Like Susan, those in slumber respond with a comment about how bliss isn't the point.

Yet, as I stated earlier, in reading the New Testament, we see that the writers repeatedly expressed the insatiable longing for their own inheritance, the hope of glory. For the bliss that awaited them.

Paul said: "I pray also that the eyes of your heart may be enlightened in order that you may know the hope to which he has called you, the riches of his glorious inheritance in the saints, and his incomparably great power for us who believe" (Eph. 1:18–19).

Although this passage is often used to encourage an awakening in this life, it is first a cry of longing directed toward the hope of our inheritance, which is the next life!

Paul's prayer is perfectly understandable—most believers *need* their eyes enlightened to the delights that await them. The eyes of their hearts are closed in a slumber to such passionate yearnings.

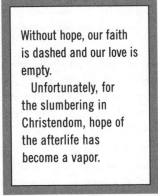

Without hope, our faith is dashed and our love is empty.

Unfortunately, for the slumbering in Christendom, hope of the afterlife has become a vapor.

The New Testament writers were inordinately taken with the word *hope*, and in particular the hope of that which was to come, since hope in that which has already happened is no hope at all (Rom. 8:24).

Yet in Christendom, we hardly know what hope means any longer. In the end there is faith, hope, and love, and the greatest of these is love. Yes, but both *faith and love spring from a hope* of heaven, according to Paul (Col. 1:5). Without hope, our faith is dashed and our love is empty.

Unfortunately, for the slumbering in Christendom, hope of the afterlife has become a vapor.

Solomon's Conclusion

Let's return to King Solomon's simple conclusion on man's search for happiness. It's true, as he stated, that there is nothing better for men to do than be happy while they live and do good, for this is God's gift to them. But we must also consider his most critical comments that lead up to this conclusion.

Here in the space of one verse, the wisest man who lived gave us a secret that must precede any attempt by man to enjoy the gifts of God. Read:

> He has made everything beautiful in its time. He has also set eternity in the hearts of men; yet they cannot fathom what God has done from beginning to end. (Eccl. 3:11)

Having said this, Solomon went on to state that we should indeed be happy while we live. But he couched our happiness in a clear announcement that true beauty will come only in its time. That life is truly about eternity, which has been stamped on the hearts of men. That even though man has difficulty understanding what God's true plan is from beginning to end, man is dependent on that plan, which focuses on eternity.

Only after he made this claim did Solomon continue. Now, he said, while we wait that end out—while we live on this earth, waiting for the eternity stamped on our hearts—let us avail ourselves of the happiness God has given us as a gift.

But what if we let eternity drift out of our focus? What if we focus instead on this life alone? What if we lose sight of God's plan from beginning to end?

Then the pleasures and benefits God has given us for this life will fail us. Yet the church has turned its eyes to the benefits of Christianity for this life, and in doing so has fallen asleep to any true passion for eternity.

Eternity has indeed been branded on our hearts, but we have been lulled into a numbing slumber, and we no longer feel the hot brand of heaven that once seared our hearts.

The results have been devastating.

A Shocking Discovery

A rather shocking thing happened to me this week. I began to urinate blood. Yes, I know this is an unusual admission to make in the middle of writing this book, but the events of the last few days fit so seamlessly with our discussion that I feel compelled to share them.

I am forty-two years old at the time of this writing, October 2004. To the best of my knowledge, males my age aren't supposed to urinate blood. For forty-two years I've taken my basic bodily functions for granted, rarely pausing to consider the wonder of breath or pulse or urination.

Yet here I am, writing a book on the pleasure and pain of this life, and the bliss of the next life, when suddenly I begin to urinate blood.

It all started a week ago after spending a few hours on my motocross bike, pounding my body on bumps and jumps no sane man my age should consider. But the doctor has assured me that no amount of slamming on a motorcycle can cause the body to urinate blood.

The pain, I must say, is excruciating.

I've done something else no sane man should consider. I've allowed them to take a look at my bladder. Now, forgive me for injecting just a bit of levity here, but I must. It helps me balance the doctor's discovery.

It seems that the source of this blood in my urine is a hematoma of some kind inside me. The doctor has never seen anything like it. He took a sample of the surrounding fluid to test for cancer.

I'm a forty-two-year-old man who has just learned that he might have cancer. Do I have two years to live? A year? Will I be dead in six months? Two months? Two weeks? Before I have a chance to finish this message God has placed on my heart? It happens, you know. They go in, find a small irregularity, and soon uncover something far worse than imagined.

There's nothing like an acute dose of your own mortality to focus your mind on the afterlife. Is God testing me? I intend to write on pain and suffering later in this book—is this some sort of trial?

You may think all these thoughts are premature—as the doctor says, bladder cancer for such a young nonsmoker would be a shock. I don't care what the doctor says, I'm the one with the spot he's never seen. My imagination is going wild on this one. More later . . .

Now it's time to rejoin my own gradual descent into the slumber of Christianity.

4

Give Me Pleasure or Give Me Death

One Man's Journey to Discover Happiness (Part Two)

Now, where were we in my story of discovery?

Oh, yes. We had reviewed my gradual descent into slumber. We had examined my unsuccessful quest for belonging and fulfillment. We were at the part where I had lost my childhood faith and slipped into disillusionment.

We were near the bottom of my life's barrel.

Or so I thought.

Without a burning passion for Christ at the close of my college years, I set my eyes on the American dream in California. I came to the deliberate determination that the only way to truly find happiness was to throw myself into the pursuit of all the world had to offer through wealth and success as defined by the world.

I took a job delivering medical supplies for a company of about two hundred employees in Long Beach. Within months I had talked my supervisors into promoting me, and I took a job behind a customer service desk. Within a few more months I had persuaded the same supervisors to let me manage a store in San Diego. Within another year I had threatened to leave unless they tripled my

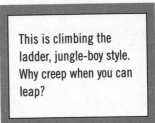

This is climbing the ladder, jungle-boy style. Why creep when you can leap?

salary and put me in charge of direct marketing at the home office, where I believed I belonged. They agreed.

This is climbing the ladder, jungle-boy style. Why creep when you can leap?

I had learned much about the world of business from the Chinese merchants in Indonesia, where only the simplest, laziest souls could not fend for themselves on the streets of trade. Applying lessons from the street, I found the market in America to be amazingly responsive.

Three years after graduating from college, I secured the most enviable position I could imagine at the time: director of marketing. Money began to flow into our bank account. Lee Ann and I were rich! We had been two missionary kids in a jungle far away, but no more. Now we were a highly successful American couple with one child, whom we named Rachelle, and a fat bank account.

Only one thing separated me from realizing my lifelong objective of finding happiness: happiness itself.

I was buying brand-new flashy red sports cars and attending parties in my new tuxedo, and I was miserable. There clearly had to be more.

More money. Yes, that had to be it. Much more money. Heaps and heaps of money—enough to sit back and retire and enjoy life on a beach somewhere. I began to work on a fantasy of living on an island in the Caribbean, with a yacht anchored just off the shore and a cool breeze bending palm trees beside my wife and me as we sipped tall, cool drinks. This was surely the life that had eluded me for so long.

Of course, this new dream would require more—much more—money. And in the United States of America, that meant amassing equity. Ownership. A successful business.

I persuaded the general manager to leave the company we worked for and start another with me, a fifty-fifty split. With matching funds of seventy thousand dollars each, we launched Comfort Care, a medical supply company that promised to deliver adult diapers to the incontinent in the privacy of their own homes.

Why adult diapers? Because, although it was a well-hidden fact, 10 percent of American women over the age of sixty-five required some form of incontinence products. And because no other company was marketing directly to these women in their homes at that time. We put our entire nest egg into one mailing. We bet the whole enchilada on one massive campaign. One hundred thousand packets dropped in the mail on one afternoon. My happiness was now in the hands of the United States Postal Service.

I spent that first week checking the mail each day and cursing my ambition and vision, which had mysteriously transformed into anxiety and fear and were now robbing me of sleep and food. Perhaps there was a good reason no other company was using direct mail to sell adult diapers. Perhaps I had just tossed seventy thousand dollars into a deep hole, never to be seen again. Perhaps I was a fool.

We received a small blue card in the mail after eight days of waiting. It said we had some mail at the post office. My partner and I drove to the Long Beach postal center, crossed our fingers, and turned in the card.

I determinedly dismissed any notion that there wasn't a God who cared for me and begged him to deliver salvation. Please, God, please let there be a few orders. Five or ten, even; just please, please. I believe; forgive my unbelief.

The postman brought out a large white carton. Then two. Then three. All overflowing with orders. We stared in shock. Arms trembling with excitement, we hauled the containers back to the warehouse, plopped them on the floor, and began to open our precious orders. It took us four hours.

The next day there were six cartons and we knew that we had struck gold. The gods of commerce had rained goodwill on us. Life was sweet, so blissfully sweet.

At least for a few weeks.

> More, more—I needed more. True happiness was just around the corner, I could feel it in my bones. In the first three months, we cleared three hundred thousand dollars in profit, and we threw an absurdly expensive Christmas party. I was reasonably happy.

More, more—I needed more. True happiness was just around the corner; I could feel it in my bones. In the first three months, we cleared three hundred thousand dollars in profit, and we threw an absurdly expensive Christmas party. I was reasonably happy.

In the first year our success expanded. We sold more than six million dollars' worth of adult diapers, and I was less happy.

By the end of the second year, we had grown to a company with an excess of a hundred employees, and I was unhappy. The money was slipping through my fingers as fast as I could get it in my hand. The cars and furniture and vacations I purchased with that money refused to deliver anything of great pleasure. I walked around in expensive suits and issued confident orders that were sure to expand our market share, but I began to suspect with a terrible amount of certainty that the American dream was a thin vapor, easily blown into oblivion on the same winds that delivered it.

In the fourth year, Medicare slashed its payment for incontinence products and our company went broke. I was miserable. The unhappiness of success was made unbearable by failure.

A Bold New World

We had managed to sock away a sizable sum of money, and my first impulse was to head off to the Caribbean and begin living the good life as planned. I'd heard about some islands called the Turks and Caicos, and I went as far as putting down a nonrefundable deposit on land there before concluding, with generous help from Lee Ann, that we weren't quite ready to enter paradise. We had two children now, Rachelle and JT, and with them a whole new set of responsibilities.

But I was determined to leave California, the land that had given me happiness and then abandoned me.

We settled on Colorado Springs. My parents were moving there, and it seemed like a reasonable place. I had enough money to build a house and buy a small struggling manufacturing business for a couple hundred thousand dollars.

Life was looking better. Happiness was once again looming, though at the ripe old age of twenty-eight I was growing hardened to this mad, passionate pursuit of pleasure that had propelled me through my first nearly three decades.

I took over the business, rounded up the twenty or so employees, and cast a new vision for the future. I really had no assurance that the ambitious plans I proposed to them would work, but I delivered the plans with utmost conviction, enough to persuade even me.

To my delight, the team responded immediately. We slashed programs and developed new ones. We struck out on a new path that we all believed would take us up the mountain to the heights of success.

It was there, in the bowels of that company, a new realization raged to the surface of my mind: *vision propels*. We all are motivated primarily by the hope of what lies ahead of us. The company had been paralyzed by the lack of vision, but by building a new hope for a brighter future, I had caused a stir of great energy among the employees that propelled the company forward. Without a vision the people would have perished, but with a vision, they would conquer the world.

My vision wasn't particularly insightful. I am sure that any one of a dozen directions would have suited the business just fine. But the passion I managed to inject into that vision began paying huge dividends.

We humans are built for hope. Without it, we slumber and die. With it, we live and thrive. We managed to double profits within twelve months, at which time I sold the company for nearly four times what I had paid for it.

Thrilled by my success, I repeated the process. I found other struggling businesses that I could believe in, injected them with passionate vision, and raised them from the dead before selling them at significant profits. The power of vision and hope was astounding. People seemed desperate to follow any passionately cast hope.

All fine and good, but what of my own search for happiness? What vision was propelling me? What were my hopes? Happiness, of course. Yes, but how? What hope could quicken my sense of well-being where loads of money and red sports cars and vacations to the Caribbean had failed?

By this point in my life I had been through enough soul-searching and people watching to uncover an ugly truth: the more success humans find, the less happy they tend to be. And I knew why as well. Once the dream filled you with hope, and this hope drove you with enough energy to frighten those around you. Then you achieved the dream. And you discovered that the dream did not satisfy. So you pursued another dream, and achieved that dream, but it failed to give you any lasting happiness as well.

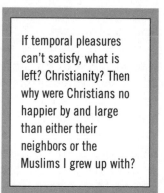

If temporal pleasures can't satisfy, what is left? Christianity? Then why were Christians no happier by and large than either their neighbors or the Muslims I grew up with?

It doesn't take long to start running out of dreams. How big of a church do you need to build before it is a truly successful church? How large of a business sale constitutes a truly successful transaction? How big of a house, long a vacation, large a bank account? How much wine? So many dreams are achievable, yet none satisfy. This is a horrific realization that the young people can't comprehend because it has to be experienced to be appreciated.

But if temporal pleasures can't satisfy, what is left? Christianity? Then why were Christians no happier by and large than either their neighbors or the Muslims I grew up with?

I still remember the day I fully recovered the faith of my youth. I was driving in the car, listening to a tape on Creation, when a light suddenly ignited in my mind. It was the simplest of lights, white and bright and thoroughly compelling. And it illuminated one simple truth.

God existed.

And Jesus was indeed God. And as my Creator, he had made me in his image, with circuitry designed to discover him as my Creator. My hope must be in him. Nothing else could begin to satisfy.

I know what you're thinking. Such an obvious revelation, one that I had lived with for many years as a missionary kid. True, but on that day this most fundamental truth exploded into my person with such conviction and power that I began to slam the steering wheel in my exuberance. This was it!

Who am I? A man created in God's image, of course!

Where do I belong? With God, naturally. In his presence.

I began that day a new kind of search. I knew then, as much through the failure of so many other pursuits as by his revelation to me, that God was calling me into a deep and profound fellowship with him.

> I could walk on water, I was sure of it. Not yet, but if I had the right amount of faith, I would surely be able to take a stroll on any lake.

My thirst for the Word became insatiable. I read the gospel of John, and every word seemed fresh and heavy with meaning.

My mind buzzed with possibilities that lay just beyond what I could taste, touch, hear, and see.

I could walk on water, I was sure of it. Not yet, but if I had the right amount of faith, I would surely be able to take a stroll on any lake. It was during this time that I began writing in the evenings, more as an outlet for my overactive mind than with any ambition of publishing. There seemed no better way to inform hope and vision than through stories. It was what Christ did.

But in all of this I failed to connect with God in a way that I most desperately wanted. I still lived with a certain frustration at the failing of life on earth to satisfy. Paradise was still beyond my reach.

The Mountain of Slumber

I decided to search for God in the mountains, alone, and so I did, numerous times. Perhaps if I knocked long and hard, heaven's gates would open to me. I remember the first time that I drove up to a place called Prayer Mountain, near Divide, Colorado, climbed from my flashy red sports car, and entered a small cabin that was to be my home until I awakened God from his slumber.

But the heavens were like granite that day. I did all I knew to do without the faintest whisper of response from above. For hours I read the Word that had moved me so many times. That day, not a breath.

The second day, I headed out into the fields, thinking that perhaps if I were surrounded by nature's beauty I would be able to hear a call from beyond. The grass was tall and brown. Dead. Rocks lay on the dirt, totally oblivious to my presence. Certainly not groaning in anticipation of their liberation.

There I begged God to show himself. *Speak to me, since you surely do exist. Anything will do. Just one whisper of confirmation.*

But the only whisper I heard was from the wind blowing

gently through pine trees. I felt nothing. I grew despondent. Empty and depressed.

Oddly enough, I grew terribly tired. So I lay down in the field of swaying brown grass, closed my eyes, and slipped into a slumber.

I didn't realize it then, but I was a real, live, slumbering Christian in the flesh. I had grown tired of my failure to awaken God. My hopelessness had lured me into a comforting sleep.

The sun was dipping when I awoke. I suddenly became desperate. *Show me yourself*, I cried. I began to dig at the earth with my fingers.

Show me where you are. Are you here, in this ground, hidden by the dirt?

Nothing.

I grabbed a piece of rotted wood. *Then here, in this wood. Surely there is evidence of you in this wood that you yourself made!*

Nothing. Nothing.

I felt like that bird looking for its mother in the children's book again. "Are you my mother?" I hadn't been able to find my mother as a child, and now my Father was evading me.

I was quite taken with the idea of being touched by God there and then, because that was as far as I could see. Like the impatient lover about to be wed, I was demanding the wedding now. And if the wedding couldn't happen now, then I had no hope for a wedding tomorrow, certainly no hope for a wedding twenty years from now. The thought of a wedding twenty years from now wasn't even in my mind. I was asleep to any such hope. The church didn't talk about, much less care about, such hopes, and neither did I.

I ripped away the bark and dug deep into the rotted wood,

> I ripped away the bark and dug deep into the rotted wood, and I was about to hurl the piece into the wind when something caught my eye. A tiny, nearly microscopic creature crawling from a crevice.

and I was about to hurl the piece into the wind when something caught my eye. A tiny, nearly microscopic creature crawling from a crevice.

Life! Life where I had been sure there was none.

I pulled back more bark. More tiny creatures. A whole world of them, thriving just behind the skin of this wood, unseen by any other human being before this moment. But the fact that they were unseen had no bearing whatsoever on their existence. They were real, discovered by humans or not. Very, very real.

I jumped over to a large dried-out log sticking up in the fading sun. I studied its surface. Not a single creature. I looked long and hard. Not a single stir.

Ah, but if I dug beyond the surface, past the skin . . .

Life! I knew it! I was staring at something similar to the kingdom of God, I thought. *It's here, I just can't see it. I can't feel it. For all practical purposes, it doesn't even exist for me.*

I walked back to the cabin, feeling as depressed as I can ever remember feeling. My faith and knowledge of God's kingdom had become unshakable in the many months leading up to this moment, but I wasn't interested in knowing. I wanted to touch, to taste, to feel that kingdom!

I lost track of time as I sat at my desk reading the Word. It wasn't speaking to me. I stared out at the fading light and watched darkness shut down day. It was deathly quiet outside. I was alone. A lost child in search of his father.

I lowered my eyes and resumed reading Isaiah chapter 1. What happened in that moment, I still can't adequately describe to this day. By now you know that I was no stranger to isolation and plumbing the depths of my mind and soul and spirit, so I can't say that my environment had much to do with what transpired next. But for no particular reason, the verse I was reading seemed to leap from the page and sear my mind.

I can't remember what verse it was—that wasn't the point. Something had changed in the room. I lifted my eyes and blinked. The place seemed to be charged with an electrical current.

Once again I lowered my eyes and began to read. The words flowed into my mind with stunning power, and I began to cry softly. Heaven was raining on me.

I read more, and what had been a rain suddenly became a waterfall, thundering down from heaven, crashing over my head with a power that shook my body. I tilted my head toward the ceiling, slumped in the chair, and began to sob loudly enough to scatter the tiny creatures on the rotten logs outside.

My Father was talking to me.

He was reaching down from heaven and whispering a few words into my ear. But to me it felt like the Atlantic Ocean was pouring over my body. I sat in that chair for hours, unable to stop the flood. I continued to read from Isaiah, but now every word screamed with power and meaning that mere mortals couldn't possibly comprehend. I read the same passage today and feel nothing of what I felt then, so I know this is true.

I can't remember anything else that happened that weekend; the rest of my time is still overshadowed by this one blessed visitation from my Father. For a month, I walked on clouds. I would walk into church, any church, and begin to cry for no reason. Everything had come alive to me. The trees, the roads, the cars— a bird could chirp over my head, and I would shed a tear of joy.

And the music. I could not finish any worship song I started. My throat would seize up midword and I would sit like a helpless puppy, overcome by emotion.

I would say that I lived in heaven for a month, but I know this isn't entirely true. Instead, I tasted heaven, and that one taste nourished me for a month.

And then a strange thing happened. The feelings faded. Gradually my former life once again became the norm. I tried to solicit another bath from heaven, but the heavens had been plugged up. Slowly, gradually, over the course of many months, my passion for that generous gift was once again overshadowed by the reality of this life.

I visited the mountain again, a different mountain this time.

Once again I was blessed, though not in the same way. Once again the experience faded. Like all good food and all fore-tastes of glory divine, the nourishment passed. And the wonder of it all began to fade.

I wanted more, but I couldn't find more. And eventually I began to once again tire of my search for this kind of happiness. It's not unlike going to the altar frequently for a couple of years and then losing confidence in the church's ability to sustain you. You see, my focus was on the immediate benefits of that experience. My focus was on the blessing to be had then and there, but those blessings invariably faded.

I was an inwardly focused Christian, consumed with the adventure set before me and frustrated with its failure to set me permanently free. I wanted to walk on the water. I wanted to fly. I wanted to laugh hysterically on my Father's lap. And I did, in some small fashion. But not as I wanted. Even these incredible experiences with God failed to satisfy me.

Do you wonder why many great leaders in the church who seem so gifted fall away? They are looking for ultimate fulfillment where none can be found, and they grow bored with ministry. The power loses its luster.

As for me, my passion gave way to a general acceptance that heaven on earth was simply not to be found, at least not by my doing.

Within a year, I again was no longer truly happy.

The Day My World Changed Forever

Recall your past and pick out a dozen primary points of impact. You might be surprised by what they reveal about you. Clearly, our lives are complex, and oversimplification undermines the beauty of our existence. But stepping back for a long look can be extremely useful.

Viewing through the lens of my search for happiness, let's summarize my life to this point. From my earliest years I wanted to belong and to be loved, because I knew this would make me happy. I set my hopes on being loved.

As I grew older this desire continued, but when the world let me down, I turned inward to create my own bubble of happiness. I set my hopes on myself, on the adventure of *this* life, and all that God had to offer me in this life.

When I was young, I searched for God to deliver me from my unhappiness and lead me into the land of happiness. I set my hopes on him but couldn't escape the nagging thought that he'd failed. Or perhaps I'd failed to impress him enough to solicit his help. Either way, Christianity delivered no lasting happiness.

In my adult years, I pursued the success of the world and grasped it, but found it empty of the true happiness I longed for. Life seemed to be a string of struggles punctuated by moments of fulfillment.

Having tasted wealth and health and most of what this world has to offer, I then turned back to a true pursuit of God. I pursued him with abandon over a long period of time that culminated on the mountaintop.

Frustrated with my inability to find heaven on earth through mountaintop experiences, I reentered the mainstream of Christianity and settled for a life less exalted than I had hoped for. In a manner of speaking, I once again fell asleep to the great pleasures of God. I went to church, I read my Bible, I led home study groups. I loved God in the same way all Christians loved God. Christ was my Savior.

But as much as this, I set my sights back on the path of earthly pleasures. Life had always been about God's blessing for me, and I set out to enjoy those blessings as best I could, despite my conviction that they would not truly satisfy me.

I bought more companies and sold them for more money. I bought more toys and houses. And above all, I drummed more vision into the minds of those souls who happened to get caught up in one of my deals. Vision and hope were without question the key to life; I had learned that much.

In the end, then, this was my life.

And then that life came to an abrupt and brutal halt.

My brother, Danny, my closest and dearest friend, shared one of my greatest passions: riding dirt bikes. The kind with motors that could throw you over a seventy-foot jump with a flick of the wrist. A small slice of heaven on earth. We had made final arrangements for a trip to the desert where we intended to tear up the sand. He'd just bored out the cylinder on his KX 250 and was thrilled with the prospect of trying out his new ride.

Our families shared tacos on the Wednesday evening before that planned weekend. Everything was set. Temporal happiness was but three short days away. We were keen on enjoying God's great gift of adventure in the wild with not one horse or two, but forty horsepower packed under our seats.

The next morning I received a phone call from my mother informing me that Danny had a light case of food poisoning and was headed to the hospital. Fine, as long as he was better by the weekend. I was headed to the western slope to look at some land to purchase. I would check in when I was settled.

But I didn't need to check in. The little red light was already flashing on top of the phone when we returned to our hotel room that evening. All four of our children, Rachelle, JT, Kara, and baby Chelise, were with us, and I hushed them as I picked up the phone and called the front desk. My sister had left a message for me to call.

I called.

Danny was dead.

The world faded to gray. I couldn't hear anything. There had to be a mistake, of course.

No, there was no mistake. Danny had contracted bacterial meningitis, and it had turned his body into a hemorrhaging mess within twenty-four hours. He was dead.

I stood from the bed and staggered outside, Lee Ann close behind. I was walking down the concrete steps to the parking lot, but I couldn't feel my legs. A pain I had never experienced swept through my body. Not the sharp physical pain caused by damaged nerve endings—nothing so benign. This was the pain of complete emptiness.

Waves and waves of anguish. There were cars in the parking lot, and Lee Ann's hand was on my shoulder, but I wasn't there. I was falling into an utter and horrible darkness.

> Waves and waves of anguish. There were cars in the parking lot, and Lee Ann's hand was on my shoulder, but I wasn't there. I was falling into an utter and horrible darkness.

Danny had left his wife, Diane, who was pregnant, and his son, Caleb. And he had left me.

For days I stumbled around in a stupor, crying like a baby without warning, in much the same way I had after heaven opened itself to me on the mountain, only now my tears were born of hell rather than heaven. I remember being surprised by the depth and resilience of the pain. It refused to give me any reprieve. I was lost again. I was alone in the dark without hope for comfort, as I had been as a child at the boarding school.

But why the pain? Why, if Danny really was in a better place? Was it my loss that caused so much pain? The fact that I had lost my only true friend? Was it the empathy I felt for Diane and her children? What was this savage beast that feasted on my heart? Did none of us who were weeping believe in the true bliss of heaven? Why weren't we throwing a party? Why, oh why such anguish?

And then with a sudden clarity, I knew. This wasn't the pain of hell. It was the pain of death. The prospect of life ending.

Yes, the other consequences of Danny's death were horrifying in themselves, but that's not what tore at me when I came face-to-face with death.

You see, if Danny had willfully left his family and me, never to be seen again, to become the king of Sardonia (a fictitious land I just now fabricated for purposes of illustration), that extremely wealthy land over the seas, north of the poorer countries, where kings have no less splendor than King Solomon himself, I would be sad, but I would not writhe in torment as I did after my brother's death. What was the difference?

In neither case would I see my brother again. In neither case would he raise his family as promised. But in the event of his becoming a wealthy king, he would have been entering a reality that was concrete and defined and full of wonders.

Through his death, on the other hand, he was entering a reality that was uninformed. It was just death. Yes, there were heaven and glory and all of that Christian talk, but nothing tangible. Nothing I had coveted or longed for were part of the reality called heaven. Heaven was hardly more than a word on a page.

My sorrow, I realized, was as much about a profound lack of passion for the afterlife and, by extension, Danny's passing into it, as about my personal loss in his going. I dealt with my brother's death by embracing what lies beyond death. Happiness is so easily defeated by death, because death is far more real to us than the bliss that follows.

The eyes of my heart were opened through the death of Danny. I began to see the world through a new set of lenses. Not the lens of Christianity, because as we will see, the religion of Christianity has failed miserably to awaken hope in a truly exotic life after death.

Instead, I began to see the world through the lens of a new and living hope, and my perspective was forever changed.

Meaning and happiness in this life are subject to meaning and happiness in the next. This was Danny's final lesson to me. My search for happiness was and is futile unless I have the bright light of eternity to show the way.

Who am I? A person destined for bliss beyond this life.

Where do I belong? There, diving deep into my Creator's lake of inexhaustible pleasures.

Am I happy? Only when I embrace hope in a glorious mansion of many rooms prepared for me. For now the Comforter will ease the pain of the Fall and offer many good blessings as foretastes of my inheritance. The blessings and the gifts of this life aren't the good news of the gospel. Our hope for life everlasting, swamped by a never-ending bliss, is the good news.

But Christianity has fallen asleep to this new and living hope. Consequently, we desperately seek satisfaction in a world where no satisfaction is to be found.

I had been writing before this time, but a new urgency to explore this hope buoyed my spirits. I had to uncover this thing the New Testament writers seemed obsessed with, and that contemporary Christianity seemed to have forgotten.

I wrote my first novel, *Heaven's Wager*, in the wake of Danny's death. I didn't care if it was published—it was meant to be written, published or not. As soon as I'd closed the cover on *Heaven's Wager*, I threw myself into *When Heaven Weeps*—a blistering testament to the pleasures that lie just behind the skin of this world.

Now, many years later, I look back and see this scarlet thread that runs through most of my novels. Lights in the dark that illuminate a banquet of delights in the dining room down the hall. Happiness. Pleasure. The greatest promise we all have as believers. The one we have forgotten about.

Hope.

My search for happiness has led me to the secret I now share with you. Life is about heaven. It is about ecstasy and great pleasure, for God is both of these. They can't truly be found here, on earth. Knowing this, Jesus sent his Comforter to ease the path between this life and the next. Among the greatest gifts offered by the Holy Spirit is hope, because without hope for the time when both ecstasy and pleasure can be found completely in God, there can be no happiness.

Ironically, once our eyes are opened to the riches of our inheritance, the blessings of this life become far richer. The colors brighter, the odors more pungent, the fabrics more textured, the fruits sweeter, the music more wondrous. It is by fixing our eyes on the light of eternity that we see clearly the pleasures of this life.

So then, this is the story of one man's search for happiness. Now we must ask the question that begs to be answered: Did I find the ultimate happiness I was looking for?

Yes and no. I found great happiness, but not on this earth. I was looking for fulfillment in this life, but with my eyes closed to the brilliant vision of eternity by which all pleasure this side of death is illuminated. I have lived most of the Christian life in a slumber to the bliss of eternity, and as a result I have been dissatisfied with that life.

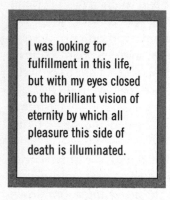

I was looking for fulfillment in this life, but with my eyes closed to the brilliant vision of eternity by which all pleasure this side of death is illuminated.

I now embrace the pleasures of this life with as much or more passion as I did before, but I do so without expecting those pleasures to provide any more than a foretaste of what is to come—a tremendously liberating knowledge.

Furthermore, I embrace those pleasures as a reminder of what is to come, without which I would undoubtedly forget and fall asleep to the promise of eternity.

Perhaps most important, I now enjoy the riches of my inheritance through a nearly miraculous power called hope. We must discover how to realize this power, and we will. Hope is our window into heaven, and we must throw back the curtains to awaken our hearts to that most spectacular view.

5

The Slippery Slope to Slumber

The Fall from Hope

Scott MacTiernan is a good friend of mine who owns San Juan Guest Ranch, a guest resort in one of the most beautiful valleys in western Colorado. At fifty, Scott is widely known throughout the industry for the first-class resort he runs and for the love he's always had for life. For many years he lived life hard and played even harder.

The poster boy for a successful sinner.

Then he fell in love with Kelly, another friend of ours. And shortly thereafter, he fell in love with Jesus.

Now, you have to understand, as anyone who knew Scott well would tell you, this Jesus thing was completely un-expected. And unlikely. From the perspective of unbelievers, there is your typical needs-Jesus kind of person, and there is your got-it-together kind of person. Scott MacTiernan was the latter.

The change in Scott was an amazing thing to watch. You'd expect a grown man of his caliber to sit quietly during the church service, soaking in the tenets of his newfound faith, not standing to testify enthusiastically about a love he could hardly put into words—at least not in typical church words.

Scott's conversion was so complete, so profound, that he hardly looked like the same hard-living man the community had known for many years. His faith was simple, and his pas-sion for Jesus was even simpler.

He had been saved. Jesus had awakened him from everlasting death and given him an everlasting life. We all watched in fascination as Scott grew in faith.

"Protect your passion," I often told him. "Whatever you do, don't let the church lull you into a slumber once again."

He would give me a puzzled look. "What do you mean?"

"Just keep your eyes on your race to the finish, not on the church," I said.

By the grace of God, Scott has remained awake. Wide awake. Five years have passed since Scott's awakening, and he now can tell you, perhaps better than I, precisely what I meant.

Let's look at this slippery slope to slumber.

The Awakening

Our journey as believers begins with an awakening.

I've always had a fascination with the beliefs of the earliest Christians. There was Christ, God himself, who lived and spoke and died to bring light into the world. We have his story and the stories he told, and they act as a plumb line for our lives.

And then there were his earliest followers, those who heard him speak and followed him around the countryside or were friends of those who followed him. How many late nights did Peter sit with Christ, discussing life in terms never recorded? What did his brother James learn growing up in the same house with Jesus?

What these early Christians heard and saw beyond what we see in the Gospels themselves is a mystery to us, but their knowledge certainly informed their writings. It is there in the writings of the early church that we see Christianity in its truest form.

So then, how did the earliest Christians, those who were intimately aware of Christ's life, characterize a person's transition from being unsaved to being saved? We have Christ's teaching in John, which describes that transition as one of rebirth, but how did the earliest Christians understand that rebirth?

Consider this song written by the early church, recorded in Paul's letter to the Ephesians: "Wake up, O sleeper, rise from the dead, and Christ will shine on you" (5:14).

Clearly those earliest believers thought of rebirth as a kind of awakening that resulted in illumination ("Christ will shine on you"). But what precisely does Christ's light illuminate in that person who has been awakened from death?

The need for him, certainly. Life abundant, more than we realize, as we will see later. Love and joy and peace, yes, yes, and yes. But these were not at the very heart of hearts of what they meant. We will see that there is more, so much more.

Consider the words of Peter, who spent nearly three years with Jesus before his death and resurrection:

> Praise be to the God and Father of our Lord Jesus Christ! In his great mercy he has given us new birth. (1 Peter 1:3)

Stop the presses. Familiar, isn't it? New birth—of course, all Christians are familiar with rebirth. Being born again is practically an American tradition. But a new birth into what? He tells us:

> Into a living *hope* through the resurrection of Jesus Christ from the dead. (v. 3, emphasis added)

Hope? Our birth is into a living *hope*? This is where most Christians' brows will furrow, when they are pressed to explain why Peter, as well as the other New Testament writers, chose such a seemingly weak word to describe the miraculous event we call salvation.

Hope sounds rather anemic, yes? It conjures notions of something less than concrete, sitting in the mind like a small light, connected to reality by a thread. But we have it wrong. Hope is far more than a flimsy notion. It's the engine of life. Peter's hope is a living hope, residing in the mind, yes, but not

> Hope conjures notions of something less than concrete, sitting in the mind like a small light, connected to reality by a thread. But we have it wrong. Hope is far more than a flimsy notion. It's the engine of life.

in an insignificant way. His hope is the source of all happiness. It is raw anticipation. Desire.

According to *The American Heritage Dictionary*, the meaning of the word *hope* is: (1) to wish for something with expectation of its fulfillment (2) to look forward to something with confidence or expectation (3) to expect and desire. The early Christian's hope was made in living by his faith, but it was still a hope. Between the hymn recorded by Paul in Ephesians and Peter's opening words in his first epistle, we have a snapshot of the early church's understanding of the gospel. I can imagine one of their campfire songs resounding with the following lyrics:

> *In his great mercy God has illuminated for us*
> *a new birth into a living hope.*
> *Wake, O sleeper, and embrace your hope.*

Do you remember the day you were awakened to this living hope? It may not have been the day you first professed faith; there is no need to limit the illumination of hope to that one moment. But at some point the scales fell from the eyes of your heart and you saw the world in a new light, unless, of course, you were born into that light as a young child.

It's difficult to describe the joy that comes with spiritual illumination to those who've never experienced it. They stare at you with a dumb look that might as well say you're a nut. Listen to any believer explain his or her conversion on the *Larry King Show*, and you know half the country is cringing. And well they should, for as Paul wrote, the gospel is foolishness to those who have not believed (1 Cor. 1:18–25).

I can hear a celebrity now on *Larry King*. "And then my life changed, Larry," he says. "I accepted Jesus Christ into my heart and became a Christian. Nothing has been the same since."

A proclamation of victory! But what most of the world hears might sound something like this: "And then my life changed, Larry. Because nothing seemed to be going right, I settled for religion. I gave up everything that used to fascinate and thrill me, crawled back to the old dead religion my grandmother used to talk about, and I finally just accepted it. But it's good. I'm okay now. No need to feel sorry for me—it's not as bad as you might think."

The guest is announcing the single most profound change conceivable, and most of the world hears something as exciting to most as a discussion on embroidery. Sadly, this includes a majority of Christians. Deep down where they don't share, they are actually embarrassed for the guest.

Have we forgotten our own salvation? For most of us who believe, that first unveiling of truth was once staggering. We may have wept with joy. We glowed with an inexpressible peace that we were desperate for. Once we were lost, but then we were found, and we wanted to shout it out from the rooftops. In fact, we did.

Even if you can't immediately recall feeling like this, you can certainly think of others who do today. You can't possibly miss them. They are the new Christians.

They're the ones bouncing off the walls in their enthusiasm while the rest of the church looks on with patient grins. *Isn't that quaint*, we all think. *Just give them time.*

No! *Don't* give them time! Stop new believers in their tracks and dig deep into their souls and uncover this mad passion that has them doing things they had never dared to do before.

In the same way I want to know what was on an early Christian's mind, I want to know what's on the new Christian's mind. But then, I already know, so I can tell you.

Hope.

Hope and more hope and heaps of hope—servings that are barely containable in the human mind.

As the hymn cries: "Blessed assurance, Jesus is mine! O what a *foretaste* of *glory divine!*"

A foretaste of glory, treasured in the heart. A desperate expectation of something just around the corner. Hope!

The good news that Jesus had borne your burden of eternal death and made a way for you to live with a new hope for eternity with him was staggering. The things of the world faded in the light of this revelation.

You were saved. Saved from what? From eternal separation from your Creator. Saved from damnation! You were a prisoner set free from the bondage of death eternal. All things became new.

And then a strange thing happened. Although you were so taken with your new life that the pleasures of the old life struck you as insignificant, your appreciation for many of those pleasures actually increased! And this was a good thing. Flowers glowed with vibrant color, and the sun shone brighter, and music sounded sweeter than you thought possible.

Nothing could stop you, because you were a joint heir with Christ, a bride awaiting the great unveiling of that heavenly wedding with eager anticipation. Christianity had delivered you into bliss.

Nothing could stop you . . .

Nothing except Christianity itself.

> Nothing could stop you, because you were a joint heir with Christ, a bride awaiting the great unveiling of that heavenly wedding with eager anticipation. Christianity had delivered you into bliss.
>
> Nothing could stop you . . .
>
> Nothing except Christianity itself.

The Slippery Slope into Slumber

Earlier I traced my own descent into slumber. Now it's time to see how you may have slipped into a similar slumber. I don't know any of the interesting details that flesh out your story— your own search for happiness, your own victories, your own disappointments—you'll have to fill those in as we go. But I can describe the most typical path that nearly all Christians take in the years following their conversions.

As the weeks ticked by after your conversion and became months, you began to notice certain subtle but odd discrepancies between your initial enthusiasm and that of those around you. Most of those who'd been Christians for a few years or more didn't seem to share your youthful exuberance for eternity. In fact, they seemed a tad put off by it. Even embarrassed.

They hardly even talked about the promise of that glorious inheritance that first attracted you. Instead, they talked about other promises. Wonderful promises for a fulfilled life here on earth. Promises of a great marriage and good health. Promises of blessing and wealth, if one would only be a good steward of that wealth.

All good things, of course. Blessings from the Father. But you couldn't help noticing a disconnect between the message that first drew you to the cross whispered by the Spirit of God, and the message that came every Sunday from the seasoned saints.

No one ever suggested that you become a Christian to earn money. No one claimed that your business would thrive if you followed Jesus. No one cried health, wealth, and success to attract you to the faith, and if they did, they birthed you into a faith inconsistent with faith in Christ. Jesus didn't come to save our bank accounts—he came to save our souls. Another chapter, another book.

As the months rolled by and became years, your own enthusiasm began to fade. And you noticed something else. For all their talk of success, the Christians around you were generally no more successful than the non-Christians you knew. In fact, perhaps less.

The most active office in the church was the counseling office. Divorce was as common among Christians as those from other faiths. Financial hardship was rampant, despite the endless promises of reciprocation if you tithed.

Worse still, most Christians talked nonstop about their struggles and characterized them as attacks from the enemy, but they never seemed to gain victory. At least not a victory that lasted longer than a week or so.

The more these Christians struggled to become happy, the more they failed to do so, and the more energy they poured into finding the key to happiness. So many sermons preached from the pulpit followed a predictable template that looked something like this: *Yes, yes, I know you're not there yet, but if you'll just follow these five points that all start with an R, your marriage and your job and your relationships and everything else in your life will improve. Rejuvenate, Restore, Remotivate, Reanimate, and Regurgitate.*

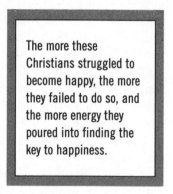

The more these Christians struggled to become happy, the more they failed to do so, and the more energy they poured into finding the key to happiness.

Bookstores overflowed with Christian versions of self-help books that dealt with the problems we all face this side of death. Or in death itself. How to live a fantastically happy life by following steps. How to heal the marriage and fix the kids and sock away money—all the things that lead to success and well-being.

These were certainly important subjects deserving of thought, but in the end you couldn't help noticing that they really didn't make the Christian that much happier. Despite the fact that most Christians had heard hundreds of sermons on how to employ God's power to have a happy marriage, their marriages weren't significantly more successful than the marriages of Muslims or Buddhists or Mormons or Hindus— the lost who did not have access to the treasure afforded to Christians. Why?

Sunday morning services seemed to be a time of celebration and peace that lasted an hour or two, but their power was quickly lost in the mix of life Monday through Saturday. Christians seemed to be addicted to the services as a reprieve from normal life, but they were rarely transformed by the promise the sermons made to better their lives.

You found yourself slowly becoming more and more like the other Christians. You, too, stopped talking about your great awakening, not because you'd forgotten that day, but because it no longer carried the luster it once had. You, too, began to seek the earthly blessings from your Father that consumed other Christians. You, too, were no longer content to rest on the great inheritance that had once awed you.

Your new and living hope for eternity began to slip into a slumber.

This is a path familiar to most modern Christians. But the path

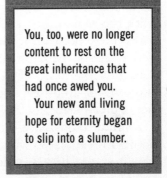

You, too, were no longer content to rest on the great inheritance that had once awed you.

Your new and living hope for eternity began to slip into a slumber.

doesn't end there. At this point, you followed one of two paths that often became the same path. One, the path followed by those who settle into a never-ending pursuit of God's blessings for this life, or two, the path of those who saw the obvious disconnect and began to lose faith in Christianity altogether.

If you are a part of the *first* group, then you probably rarely think of your faith in terms of hope for an afterlife. To you, Christianity is about the benefits of this life. You've been disappointed with your faith and found your life powerless in the face of countless challenges, but you still cling to the faith, thinking that one day you'll get your act together and really begin to live a fulfilled Christian life, reaping all the rewards that come with doing so. Although you don't know it, you're in a slumber, and you need to be reawakened to a new and living hope that has little to do with this life.

This group is as heavily populated by ministers of the gospel as those to whom they minister. Many missionaries and pastors and teachers have become so focused on widening the path to salvation and being sensitive to the seeker's tastes that they have forgotten where the path leads and what the seeker's need really is. In reality, the path is narrow, but it leads to a bliss hardly comprehensible. This gospel has gone missing.

Whether clergy or pew sitter, this group of Christians treats faith as a means to an end, and that end is found here on earth, not in heaven.

It's the rapid growth of the *second* group—those who are losing their faith altogether—that is most alarming. Surely you've seen it, perhaps most obviously among those in their teens and twenties. They tend to dangle their true beliefs and emotions for all to see, and what we see dangling isn't always such a pretty sight.

Youthful exuberance for the gospel is an irresistible magnet. But now we are faced with a pervasive lethargy among the next generation of Christians that most accurately mirrors the slumber of Christianity in this generation. You see it behind their eyes and by what they don't do, more than through open rebellion.

You see it in their boredom with Christianity.

I am speaking in gross generalizations that may offend some, but I'm doing so only to make a point. "Ted's obviously never attended a youth group like ours!" you're crying. "Asleep? We're thriving!"

True, there are many youth who are filled with a much greater awe of their true inheritance in heaven than with the latest form of entertainment. The International House of Prayer in

Kansas City, for example. Founded by Mike Bickle, IHOP is a ministry to youth and adults alike that has a profound focus on heaven and the wedding feast that awaits the bride. Walk into IHOP any hour of any day of any week of any month, and you will find anywhere from several dozen to a thousand worshippers enthralled with the beauty of the Bridegroom, Christ.

But the Christianity that attracts young people is the Christianity of earthly benefits, not the Christianity of an inheritance in heaven. Speak to many young people about our inheritance in heaven, and you'll get blank stares. They certainly won't dive into a mosh pit to express their delight with the prospect of Christ in heaven.

It's a Christianity more enamored with a good time on road trips and summer missions and great youth meetings filled with entertaining presentations of the same message being spoken in the main sanctuary than with a one-way ticket to eternity.

It's a Christianity that likes to grind to Christian music and wear Christian labels and repent for yesterday's wrongs rather than meditate on the ecstasy to come.

It's a Christianity that rolls at an altar at the beginning of the service and then rolls a joint at the end. A Christianity totally and unapologetically enamored with the foretaste of glory but with only a passing thought of glory itself.

And in the end, it is a Christianity that culminates in disillusionment, lethargy, boredom, and unbelief. One thing young people can sniff out is hypocrisy, and the same religion that once drew them often sends them packing. At some point they see that Christians really aren't that much happier than anyone else. For all the talk, their walk is the same as those who don't have the talk.

The adults nod their heads at my characterization of the younger generation, thinking it may be the best point I've made thus far, but in reality the adults are like the youth.

Or more accurately, the youth are like the adults.

It's no mystery why so many are losing their faith in this day of slumbering hope. We were saved from death into a living hope—without that hope, we slip back into a kind of death.

No form of Christianity stripped of hope can satisfy.

Put to Sleep by Christianity

Perhaps now would be a good time to direct your thoughts back to the questions I first asked of your own predicament:

- Are you desperately longing for heaven?

- Are you groaning for the day of your final redemption?

- Are you obsessed with the riches that are piling up for you on that glorious day of your death?

- Do you share Paul's sentiment that to live is Christ, but to die is gain?

- Are you, the bride of Christ, pacing the church aisle in eager anticipation of the imminent wedding?

- Has your hope slipped into a slumber?

- Have you been swallowed by a Christianity that focuses on this life more than the next?

- Is the hope of heaven ignored in your church?

> Worldly Christianity is simply heavenless Christianity.
>
> In so many teachings and books designed to prod us into successful Christian living, there's a preoccupation with life on earth.
>
> In many ways we have become our own greatest enemy.

If your answer to the last question is yes, trust me, you're not alone. The dungeons of repressed hopes are crowded by millions of Christians. And it is the religion of Christianity itself that has lulled them to sleep.

Worldly Christianity is simply heavenless Christianity.

It's a form of godliness, stripped of the power of hope. In so many teachings and books designed to prod us into successful Christian living, there's a preoccupation with life on earth rather than the life to come. In many ways, we have become our own greatest enemy.

The Machine

Let me characterize the critical nature of hope through a contemporary parable. In fact, to mix things up a bit, let's make it a futuristic parable.

Imagine a huge machine, built like a three-story glass building, in the middle of a white desert. In fact, when you first stumble upon it while crossing the desert, you think it is a building. It's black and square, like an office tower. A monolith that looks as though it may have been dropped off on the last alien flyby.

You approach the monstrosity cautiously, and once confident that it's harmless, you try to enter. It's locked tight. Being quite resourceful, you blow the door with some handy TNT. After the smoke clears you enter.

Dark. Pitch-black, in fact. You pull out a large flashlight and flip it on. The beam of light reveals gears and gadgets that fill you with awe. You slowly work your way into the building and discover that every room contains new gadgets, each seeming to have its purpose. If only you could figure out what they were for or, better yet, how to turn them on.

You set up camp outside and begin a careful examination of the building, which you now recognize as a machine of some kind. At the very least a series of machines, all housed in one structure for some apparent reason. For days you fiddle with the gears and toy with the gadgets. You manage to turn a few of them on and are delighted to discover that they actually work.

Others come and begin to explore with you. No one can

figure out what the machine is for and how it works, but some of the rooms have small systems that reveal their functions. One produces water and another cranks out gold. There is a huge contraption on the tenth floor that looks like an engine of some kind, but no amount of tinkering can bring it to life.

Soon a town sprouts up around the machine. Each day more discoveries are made. Conflict erupts over who should own the gold and control the water, and the growing community institutes regulations and laws to manage that conflict. Claims are filed, and over time a thriving commerce develops around the machine.

The town becomes a city in the desert. The machine is a wonder to all who enter the doors. A use is eventually made for every gadget and gear. The wonder from the sky is the talk of the world.

Still, no one can figure out how to turn on the machine. Like ants, thousands scurry in and out of the monolith all day, but the structure itself stands in darkness, slumbering. Years go by, and soon any notion of waking the slumbering giant is forgotten.

One night while the city sleeps, you make a fascinating discovery on the tenth floor: a large pearl, roughly the size of your fist, hidden on top of the silent contraption that looks like an engine. The pearl looks priceless, and you're sure this is a treasure that will make you rich beyond measure.

Then it occurs to you that you've seen something like this pearl before. A drawing of a similar pearl in one of the contraption's openings.

You eagerly climb down and pull open the hatch in question. Sure enough, there is a drawing that looks identical to the pearl in your hand. You place the pearl in what appears to be a receptacle made for it.

Nothing happens. Beside the drawing there is a switch. What if . . .

You flip the switch.

In an instant your world changes. Blinding light floods the room, and a whirl deafens your ears. The floor begins to hum loudly, and you think the whole contraption might blow up.

Terrified, you tear down the stairs as the building comes to life around you. Gears spin and gadgets roar to life, breaking any clumsy, man-made construction built to harness their power.

By the time you break through the front door, midnight has been turned to day. Light streams from the glass building and floods the surrounding desert.

You stand in awe at a safe distance now, watching with a thousand others. Without a shred of doubt, the spectacle unfolding before your eyes is something that could come only from heaven itself.

The next day you brave your way back into the glowing machine. The wonders you discover inside are indescribable.

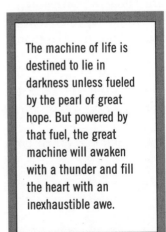

The machine of life is destined to lie in darkness unless fueled by the pearl of great hope. But powered by that fuel, the great machine will awaken with a thunder and fill the heart with an inexhaustible awe.

The glory of this machine makes all the efforts of many technicians, who've spent years putting the machine to good use, seem juvenile and silly by comparison.

The path of wondrous discovery that lies ahead of you is surely mind-bending. What mystery does the machine really hold? How can such a great power be contained by glass? What kind of being made such a magnificent machine?

And to think you once tried to make bread with this thing.

The end.

The machine is the heart of happiness, placed in every man and woman and child by God himself. Though it once was full of life, it has slipped into a slumber and sits in darkness.

The pearl is the hope of eternity, which fuels the machine and brings it to life.

No matter how man will find pleasure within its gears and contrive usefulness from its gadgets, the machine of life is destined to lie in darkness unless fueled by the pearl of great hope. But powered by that fuel, the great machine will awaken with a thunder and fill the heart with an inexhaustible awe.

Happy is the man who finds this pearl of great price.

Awakening

What falls asleep can be awakened. This is the hope held out to all who have lost that first love.

Although change rarely comes with the flip of a switch, realization often does. And with realization, hope. Like the machine in our parable, finding new hope in a rekindled passion for God can happen now, even as you read this paragraph. It begins with the illuminating power of the Holy Spirit filling the dark corners of your mind with truth. One of these truths may very well be that you, too, have slipped into slumber. You, too, have lost your inner groaning for heaven.

Although we will deal with awakening from slumber in far greater detail in the second half of the book, if you're at all responsive to what has been presented thus far, you're likely already beginning to awaken.

Open your eyes. Acknowledge your slumber. Awaken new hope.

6

In Living We Die; In Dying We Live

Facing the Truth of Our Faith

Nearly a week has passed since the doctor found the spot on my bladder, and no word. Evidently the test is lengthy. Or perhaps they know whether or not I have cancer and are thinking through the best way to break this horrible news.

The bleeding is gone, and I'm on a heavy dose of antibiotics despite no sign of infection in the culture they did earlier. When I imagine my own death, an odd peace swallows me, but I am afraid for my wife and children. I have four children, and the youngest is only seven.

The most recent history of my seven-year-old daughter still reverberates through my mind. Her name is Chelise, and she is a treasure I can't begin to describe. She sings and dances, and she makes me sing and dance.

A few months ago she was diagnosed with JMDS, an extremely rare autoimmune disease that attacks the skin and muscles (only a handful of cases are reported each year). There is no cure. Although she's gone into remission with heavy doses of prednisone, the body normally takes two years to send the disease into permanent remission. We pray earnestly that it does—I can't imagine harm coming to her.

But it's not just her disease that bothers me. It's the fact that I wrote a story earlier this year about a girl who was part of a race that suffered from a skin disease in a novel called *White*. The story uses a device in which spiritual realities manifest themselves in physical form. A story in which whatever is written in certain books becomes reality.

Strangely enough, I had named the girl in my novel Chelise, my daughter's name. It's as if my story has become flesh, just like those in my novel.

I don't assume that either my or my daughter's condition is a direct result of my writing, but believe me, my mind has been more acutely focused on the unseen as of late.

I also have learned that even if the reports from last week's test come back negative, they want to take another look in five weeks. If the abnormality still remains, they will do further tests.

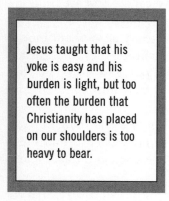

Jesus taught that his yoke is easy and his burden is light, but too often the burden that Christianity has placed on our shoulders is too heavy to bear.

So, then, this question lingers: When will I die? According to King Solomon, that time has been appointed. I don't want to be morbid; I just want to be realistic.

Now is a good time to consider what our faith in Jesus Christ really says about death. We must delve deep into the Word to uncover God's message about life and death and hope after death.

One factor that has led to our slumber is bad theology. Or worse, no theology, no true understanding of God's perspective on death, no appreciation for what the writers of the New Testament had to say about this faith we call Christianity.

It is critical that we have a clear theology of both death and hope.

Bear with me, because in the end we will find some great freedom in this discussion.

Born to Die

Jesus taught that his yoke is easy and his burden is light, but too often the burden that Christianity has placed on our shoulders is too heavy to bear. Misguided theology can burden us with an expectation of more earthly fulfillment and satisfaction than we will realize.

We expect perfect bliss in our marriages here on earth when such a bliss isn't available, at least not here.

We beg God for better jobs, but none come.

We trust for growth in our churches, but the numbers stagnate.

And when we don't find these expected benefits to our faith, we begin to falter.

We must dump the loads of expectations for nirvana in this life along with the burden of finding ultimate happiness. That happiness simply isn't available during our allotted eighty-odd years. The bliss we seek awaits in the *next* life. Our faith is being sure of this hope. The pleasures God has given us serve as a reminder of far greater pleasures to come.

Understanding this truth will liberate you in a way you never knew possible. So then, let us see if the Scriptures really do teach what I am suggesting they teach.

In living we die; in dying we live. Speak this from a pulpit and the congregation will absently stare up at you. But when pressed, everyone seems to agree. Yes, of course, by living we eventually die, and when we die we eventually will get around to living some kind of glorious life.

Do you want to die or do you want to live?

I want to live! you say.

And how do you live—really, really live?

A long pause.

Isn't it true that only after we die will we truly live, with Christ?

What are you saying, that I should think of suicide so that I can really, really live instead of just plain old living?

No. But perspective is critical if we are to awaken from our current slumber.

There is one thing in your life that will necessarily lead to death. Living. Not cigarettes, alcohol, Twinkies, or preservatives, but breathing and walking and being alive. These will age you and ultimately kill you no matter what you do. You can add or shave a few years depending on how often you exercise and what you eat, but generally speaking, you have eighty or so years to do your thing, and then you're gone.

Death is the destiny of every man. (Eccl. 7:2)

In living we die. But don't fear, because in dying we live! Then why do we sweep death under the rug?

In Living We Die

In its obsession with happiness and life, our culture has locked death in a closet and tried desperately to lose the key. We certainly don't treat death as the doorway into bliss. Naturally, we soothe the wounds of those affected by death by prescribing the notion of a better place that awaits us. But we do so as a kind of anesthetic to deal with the pain of death rather than a belief that motivates us apart from death.

Eternity has become more of a crutch in Christianity than a prize.

Growing up in a Stone Age culture that was deeply spiritual,

> In its obsession with happiness and life, our culture has locked death in a closet and tried desperately to lose the key. We certainly don't treat death as the doorway into bliss.

I saw that death was an event terribly feared by the tribes. But it wasn't hidden. On the contrary, a death was announced with loud mourning and a blazing fire that lit the night sky.

The difference between them and us is that they had a vibrant belief in the afterlife, prompting them to make much about a loved one's passing into it. We, for all our talk, don't have such a well-informed belief in the afterlife, so we try to hide it. Our penchant for life on earth has driven us to embrace it on every level imaginable and to denounce anything that might interfere with that life.

Consider our culture's abhorrence of violence as one example of our preoccupation with life. The number of well-intending Christian parents who shield their children from any kind of violence in movies while turning a blind eye to sexual promiscuity has always amazed me. We live in one of the most nonviolent cultures on earth, and yet we fear violence more than most cultures.

Take a peek into any of the cultures in New Guinea where I grew up. Take a casual glance down through history, at the Civil War, World War II, the Flood. Glance ahead at the Apocalypse to come and war waged by heaven to destroy life on earth.

We live in a Christianity that wears Paul's admonishment to *think on whatever is true, whatever is lovely, whatever is admirable* (Phil. 4:8) as a kind of spiritual badge that endorses our preoccupation with happiness on earth, without recognizing that certain kinds of violence and death clearly fall into the category of things to which we ought to turn our minds.

The unending violence depicted in the holy Scriptures is something we should think about regularly. We are urged to meditate on all Scripture, including the many horrifying metaphors cast by the prophets, which are enough to make any civilized person cringe. And on the passion of Christ. These all are things we ought to bring our minds to and think about regularly.

I'm sure God could fill a million thick volumes with revelation about the world and how we ought to live in it. But he chose to put whatever revelation we needed in one book. The Word of God. You must ask yourself, why is so much of that book about violence and death? Isn't God civilized? Surely he could have found a gentler way of countering evil.

Let me be clear then. Our fears of physical death and all those things that lead to death come from the Fall, not from God. Our enemy has turned death into something to be feared and, by extension, swept under the rug. But when you sweep death under the rug, you will likely sweep the afterlife under the rug with it. By hiding death, you hide the afterlife, and by hiding the afterlife, you hide any hope you have in it.

> When you sweep death under the rug, you will likely sweep the afterlife under the rug with it. By hiding death, you hide the afterlife, and by hiding the afterlife, you hide any hope you have in it.

When your hope is hidden, it falls asleep.

A Simple Theology of Death

Of the dozens of references to death in the New Testament, most are about the second death, which is *spiritual* death. There are many good explanations of this, but none as concise as John's in the book of Revelation:

> The lake of fire is the *second death*. If anyone's name was not found written in the book of life, he was thrown into the lake of fire [the second death]. (20:14–15, emphasis added)

The first death, or physical death, was nothing of terrible concern to the writers. The second death, on the other hand, seemed to be a daily topic of concern.

"Who will rescue me from this body of death?" asks Romans 7:24. And the answer? *Christ*.

Spiritual death was a thing to be feared, which explains why Paul wrote tirelessly on the subject. The world lives in spiritual death, but through Christ we are born again into a new life. Not a new physical life, but a new spiritual life that makes physical death irrelevant.

Paul's entire theology was seen through the lens of spiritual death's being conquered by Christ.

> We were therefore buried with him through baptism into death in order that, just as Christ was [physically] raised from the dead through the glory of the Father, we too may live a new [spiritual] life. (Rom. 6:4)

We know Paul refers to death as a spiritual death not only by context, but by his proclamation in 1 Corinthians 15 of what will happen after the world as we know it has ended and we all are physically dead: "The last enemy to be destroyed is death" (v. 26).

Physical death has already occurred here. He's referring to a spiritual death, from which we will be spared. And yet too many Christians follow the world's lead and think of physical death when they consider the subject of death in general.

Paul goes even further in his letter to the Corinthians, scoffing at those concerned with what happens to the physical body at death. His tone is dismissive, and his words are ripe with frustration at such petty thinking. "How foolish!" he cries (1 Cor. 15:36). And then in the next ten verses:

> Don't you realize that the body is like a seed, planted in the ground? It dies, and no one cares what it looks like. It must die to live. But what comes from that seed is far more glorious. We, like a seed, are put in the ground and perish in a small, inconsequential way. But we, like the seed that grows into a magnificent tree, are raised with power and glory as spiritual beings. (vv. 37–46, author's paraphrase)

Paul ends his lengthy discourse on death with the familiar verse common among the Christians of his day, likely the words to an early church hymn:

> Death has been swallowed up in victory.
> Where, O death, is your victory?
> Where, O death, is your sting?
> (1 Cor. 15:54–55)

It's almost as if Paul is saying, *Listen, you fools* (his choice of words, not mine), *don't you realize that the true sting of death is sin, which is a spiritual death, not this seed we call a body?!*

Fear of Death?

The death that we, along with Paul, should fear is spiritual death. Christ admonished us to fear the one who can kill the soul, not just the body.

Yet we seem to have it backward. We tend to go to extremes to protect the body rather than the soul. And it's no wonder, really. The god of this world knows all too well the devastating nature of spiritual death. He's gone to great lengths to distract us from that death by redirecting our fears of death to *physical* death. He began by slaughtering Christ. Then he continued by killing as many of Christ's followers as he could, intending to strike fear into their hearts.

I have been criticized on occasion for depicting violence and death in some of my novels. But unless we, as Christians, haul this toothless monster out of his corner and thrust him into the bright light, he will sow fear as he always has.

We Christian writers must paint evil with the blackest of brushes, not to sow fear, but to call out the monsters to be scattered by our light. If Satan cloaks himself as an angel of white, intent on deceiving the world, any attempt on our part to minimize evil is only complicit with his strategy. I can see the *un*enlightened doing this, but us? No.

Turn to the light; don't fear the shadows it creates.

Fear of death is Satan's playmate. Consider this admonishment to the Hebrews:

> Since the children [humans] have flesh and blood, he [Christ] too shared in their humanity so that by his death he might destroy him who holds the power of death—that is, the devil—and free those who all their lives were held in slavery by *their fear of death*. (2:14–15, emphasis added)

In their dark prison of repressed hope, too many Christians have once again submitted themselves to the fear of death, which enslaves them.

I am not suggesting that there is no place for sorrow in regard to death. I'm not suggesting that any Christian who does anything but laugh hysterically in joyful celebration at the passing of a loved one should be soundly whipped.

On the contrary, we should feel sorrow for our loss. Jesus wept at his friend's death. Paul stated clearly that "godly sorrow brings repentance that leads to salvation and leaves no regret, but worldly sorrow brings death" (2 Cor. 7:10).

Clearly there is a place for sorrow. But do you see how it all works? Godly sorrow is embraced by those who have no regret at a person's physical death because they know that salvation awaits. But worldly sorrow brings nothing except death.

In Dying We Live

Having now seen what the attitude of the New Testament writers was toward death, and having suggested that the prevailing attitude in the church is at odds with their attitude, we must ask the next logical question: *Why?*

Why are we afraid of death? Why has our focus been shifted from a certain carelessness about life to a preoccupation with extending this life?

By now you know what I will say. We Christians, like the world, are so taken with this life full of all its colors and sounds and tastes that give us joy, we don't really want the next life, which, as far as we can see, consists of nothing more than playing harps around a throne. It's no wonder we don't want to die.

But in all truthfulness, Christianity is about dying. Not only about dying to sin, but about living after death, which requires a physical death.

To say that physical death was embraced by the early Christians is an overstatement, but to say that the hope of life after death minimized death surely isn't. When you think about it, the two are similar. If you are eagerly awaiting life after death, you are by default anxiously awaiting death.

You might not be too excited about the means by which you die, but the prospect of stepping into the long-awaited promise after your death is an enticing prospect, indeed.

I've said that without an inflamed hope for eternity, Christians slip into a terrible slumber. I've illustrated that slumber and the power of hope to awaken the machine of happiness, and I've suggested that we were created to be happy but can't possibly be, unless we are filled with hope. But none of these claims can hold water unless they are abundantly evident in the Word that lights our path.

Even in Christian doctrine, trends come and go. One year it's spiritual warfare, the next it's a prayer by Jabez, and still the next it's some form of generational bondage. Which doctrines should act as the true plumb lines of our faith?

The one prevailing word of advice I have given my children as they've tested the shifting doctrinal winds is to stand back and review the writings of the apostles. If any particular principle was critical to following Christ, surely the writers would have not only written about it, but written fairly extensively about it, assuming that it was an issue of their day. We all grow weary of entire doctrines being lifted from one or two obscure references.

In following my own advice, I have no intention of hanging any of my claims on the odd reference or two. Gladly, I don't have to. The Word is stuffed to overflowing with the subject at hand—Hope.

And yet, it is undoubtedly one of the most misunderstood terms in the Bible. The ignorance has aided our slumber.

Expressing the Inexpressible

Let's return to Peter's first letter. The first two verses are salutation. Then he summarized the gospel, a truth on which all of what he was about to say hung:

> Praise be to the God and Father of our Lord Jesus Christ! In his great mercy he has given us new birth into a living hope through the resurrection of Jesus Christ from the dead. (1 Peter 1:3)

Yes, yes, we've already covered this. We see his obvious emphasis on Christianity being a faith based on birth into a living hope. But now it's time to unveil the rest of the story. He didn't stop there. Hope in what? Next verse:

> And into an inheritance that can never perish, spoil or fade— kept in heaven for you. (v. 4)

Stop! Digest. Do you hear Peter? He said something quite bold here. He said that our hope is for an inheritance, not on this earth, but kept in heaven for us. And more, he has suggested that whatever is kept in heaven is different from what God has given us here in that it won't spoil or fade.

In his summary of our faith, Peter undermined all that we

try to cherish on earth and pointed to everything we can't yet taste, touch, or see. How disappointing in an age when we want, we need, we demand everything now.

But we *do* have something now. New birth! Into a living hope.

Hope? How boring is that? Not nearly as boring as you might imagine. But there is more to Peter's lengthy summary of our salvation. Let's continue.

> You, who through faith are shielded by God's power until the coming of the salvation that is ready to be revealed in the last time. (vv. 4–5)

My, my, what on earth was he saying? That our salvation won't even be revealed until the end? That's exactly what he said. We are indeed saved, but that salvation won't be totally revealed until after we die. In the meantime, we have great power through faith to sustain and protect us, but the goal is eternal bliss, not fading pleasure. There's more.

> In this [salvation at the end] you greatly rejoice, though now for a little while you may have had to suffer grief in all kinds of trials. These have come so that your faith—of greater worth than gold, which perishes even though refined by fire—may be proved genuine and may result in praise, glory and honor when Jesus Christ is revealed. (vv. 6–7)

Not only are the gifts of this world subject to spoiling and the pleasures to fading, but Peter is saying that we can expect grief and trials here. But not to worry, because it all will be worth it later, when Jesus Christ, our salvation, is revealed.

Clearly the Christians that Peter was writing to were under persecution, as Jesus promised we all would be. But there is no apology made for this. From the beginning, the persecution was as expected as the bliss that awaited them.

Just a little more and we have a clear picture of Peter's Christian mind-set. The next verses bring his theology to a climax:

> Though you have not seen him, you love him; and even though you do not see him now, you believe in him and are filled with an inexpressible and glorious joy, for you are receiving the goal of your faith, the salvation of your souls. (vv. 8–9)

Case closed. We don't see him, but we believe and are filled with inexpressible joy for what? For the goal of our faith, which we are in the process of receiving. Salvation. Heaven. A taste now and bliss eternal just around the corner!

Christianity's foundation rests on a living hope that fills us with an inexpressible joy for that which is to come. Without this hope, our faith will fail, we won't have the power to withstand our trials, and we will slip into a slumber.

Would now be a good time to repeat those few probing questions that help us gauge our own hope? Just how inexpressible is *our* joy at the prospect of heaven?

Inexpressible, perhaps, but because we're snoring through it all. How can we express anything in our sleep?

Groaning Through Life

If you think Peter was a lone voice to the Jews and might have been overstating the case, you haven't read Paul. Read:

> We rejoice in the hope of the glory of God. Not only so, but we also rejoice in our sufferings, because we know that suffering produces perseverance; perseverance, character; and character, hope. And hope does not disappoint us. (Rom. 5:2–5)

Here it is again, just like Peter's verses, all wrapped up in one nice little package. We rejoice in what? Hope. Not hope in an easy road paved wide by the good news that Christ came to set us free from difficulties, but the hope of glory. An eager expectation of that which will be unveiled, after this life. In fact, he set an agenda for hardships by stating that although this world will bring us suffering, it's okay, because that suffering leads us back to the grand prize. Hope.

And hope will not disappoint. Seal the envelope, put a stamp on it, and send this down to Rome.

Paul wrote something similar in his opening words to the Christians in Ephesus, which I've already quoted from once:

> I pray also that the eyes of your heart may be enlightened in order that you may know the hope to which he has called you, the riches of his glorious inheritance in the saints. (Eph. 1:18)

There can be no mistake, even for a third grader. Christ has called us to hope in a very rich and glorious bliss, and this is our inheritance.

More? Consider just a few references from the New Testament:

- Be joyful in *hope*, patient in affliction, faithful in prayer. (Rom. 12:12, emphasis added)

- May the God of *hope* fill you with all joy and peace as you trust in him, so that you may overflow with hope by the power of the Holy Spirit. (Rom. 15:13, emphasis added)

- Those also who have fallen asleep in Christ are lost. If only for this life we have *hope* in Christ, we are to be pitied more than all men. (1 Cor. 15:18–19, emphasis added)

- By faith we eagerly await through the Spirit the righteousness for which we *hope*. (Gal. 5:5, emphasis added)

- I eagerly expect and *hope* that I will in no way be ashamed, but will have sufficient courage so that now as always Christ will be exalted in my body, whether by life or by death. For to me, to live is Christ and to die is gain . . . I am torn between the two: I desire to depart and be with Christ, which is better by far; but it is more necessary for you that I remain in the body. (Phil. 1:20–24, emphasis added)

- We always thank God . . . because we have heard of your . . . faith and love that spring from the *hope* that is stored up for you in heaven. (Col. 1:3–5, emphasis added)

- Since we belong to the day [the light of salvation], let us be self-controlled, putting on faith and love as a breastplate, and the *hope* of salvation as a helmet. For God did not appoint us to suffer wrath [hell] but to receive salvation through our Lord Jesus Christ. (1 Thess. 5:8–9, emphasis added)

- Paul, an apostle of Christ Jesus by the command of God our Savior and of Christ Jesus our *hope*. (1 Tim. 1:1, emphasis added)

- The knowledge of the truth that leads to godliness—a faith and knowledge resting on the *hope* of eternal life, which God, who does not lie, promised. (Titus 1:1–2, emphasis added)

- Let us hold unswervingly to the *hope* we profess, for he who promised is faithful. (Heb. 10:23, emphasis added)

- Now faith is being sure of what we *hope* for and certain of what we do not see. (Heb. 11:1, emphasis added)

- We know that when he appears, we shall be like him, for we shall see him as he is. Everyone who has this *hope* in him purifies himself, just as he is pure. (1 John 3:2–3, emphasis added)

Naturally there are many aspects to the good news we as Christians profess, but at the very heart of the message is this resounding truth summarized from the verses above:

Our hope is for what is stored up for us in heaven, and in our salvation from God's wrath, and in being like him when he appears. If our hope is for only the things our faith can give us in this life, we are to be pitied more than all men! True hope purifies us and is the source of our joy through the power of the Spirit. Love and faith spring from this hope. Departing to be with Christ is better *by far* than living for him on earth. Therefore, let us hold unswervingly to the hope of the afterlife lest we fall into a slumber.

This is the heart of the gospel.

But what about the long sections of Paul's letters from which most sermons are taken? you ask. *Surely these were important to happy living! You're oversimplifying*, you say.

No, I'm focusing, and I'm doing so because the hope of glory was the focus of the New Testament church.

Think of all the *therefores* in Paul's letters. He had a pattern of asserting the heart of the gospel and then following that assertion with lengthy discourses on how we should then live. Colossians 3:1–4 is a perfect example. Paul started off with asserting the gospel:

> If our hope is for only the things our faith can give us in this life, we are to be pitied more than all men! So says Paul.

Since, then, you have been raised with Christ, set your hearts on things above, where Christ is seated at the right hand of God. Set your minds on things above, not on earthly things. For you died, and your life is now hidden with Christ in God.

When Christ, who is your life, appears, then you also will appear with him in glory.

Then Paul launched into the implications resulting from the assertion that our lives are more about things above than things in this life. Verse 5:

Put to death, *therefore*, whatever belongs to your earthly nature. (emphasis added)

So, although it's true that most of the Word's content concerns how we should live on earth, all the admonitions from which we take so many of our sermons are rooted in a profound hope of heaven.

I could easily rest my case here, but we can't stop now. There is more. The holy Scriptures are heavy with hope, and so must be our writing. Stopping now might cast the false illusion that true Christianity's preoccupation with hope for the afterlife is less than it really is.

Paul's Preoccupation

There is a tale of an old man who had climbed Mount Everest many times in his life. The cost of climbing this mountain is high, and the risk is great. Only one in three expeditions ever reach the summit, and many die in their attempts.

When returning to climb the mountain yet one more time in the twilight of his life, the old man was asked why he would risk such danger again and again. To this the old man replied:

"Obviously, you've never seen the view from the top."

Paul was one who had indeed seen the view from the top. He not only saw the light of Christ on the road to Damascus, but later in the desert he was caught up to heaven—to paradise—where he "heard inexpressible things" (2 Cor. 12:4).

Having been given a glimpse of the bliss that awaits us, Paul lived a life obsessed with that day when he would have his full inheritance. Any such encounter with that bliss will surely bend any man to a fanaticism for it. So it is no wonder that Paul was so fanatical about the hope of glory.

Grasping Paul's true penchant for hope requires that we look into chapter 8 of his letter to the Roman Christians. Here we find one of the most fascinating and succinct explanations of the Christian life. Any remaining doubts about God's design for hope in a future life will soon be gone.

Paul started with terms familiar by now, casting the shortcomings of this world as insignificant next to the hope of that which is to come:

> I consider that our present sufferings are not worth comparing with the glory that will be revealed in us. (Rom. 8:18)

Then he moved on to this staggering characterization of life:

> We know that the whole creation has been groaning as in the pains of childbirth right up to the present time. Not only so, but we ourselves, who have the firstfruits of the Spirit, groan inwardly as we wait eagerly for our adoption as sons, the redemption of our bodies. For in this *hope* we were saved. (Rom. 8:22–24, emphasis added)

It is clear. We followers of Christ have been filled with the Holy Spirit and been given the firstfruits, which provide a foretaste of what is to come. Those firstfruits consist of both earthly pleasures and small glimpses of God's great love. Yet we weren't saved for those firstfruits, but for something far greater. In fact, we suffer now, even with the help of the Holy Spirit. But then we will discover incomparable glory. This is our hope!

So great is the glory awaiting us that if we, like Paul, became fully aware of it, we couldn't help our groaning, like a woman in childbirth, desperate for that day. This is the hope of our salvation.

Paul ended his snapshot of salvation with an explanation of the nature of hope itself:

> For in this hope we were saved. But hope that is seen is no hope at all. Who hopes for what he already has? But if we hope for what we do not yet have, we wait for it patiently. (Rom. 8:24–25)

There can be no mistake about the object of our hope. It is not in what we see now. It is not in the gifts of the Spirit. It is not in a large ministry or a thriving church. It is not in a good marriage or good health or good food.

It is heaven. This is true Christianity, and this is what we were saved into. A kingdom so rich in reward, our hope for that kingdom causes us to groan.

I remember watching in horror as my wife gave birth to our first daughter. Being a real trouper, she'd decided to dispense with the spinal block and try a natural birth. The five or ten minutes leading up to the birth were actually quite embarrassing. It was the noise, you see. The loud groans and screams. They were guttural and unnatural, issuing from a woman completely oblivious to any attempt by me or anyone else to calm her. Trying to shush her would have likely rewarded me with a fist in my gut rather than any cooperation.

In Paul's day, they had no spinal blocks. The whole village knew what childbirth was like. The screams surely woke the dead.

The birthing done in Christianity today is oddly quiet, don't you think? Where are the loud inward groans? Show me where we have cast off restraint in our desperation to enter the world awaiting us.

Being the unhelpful bystander as my wife gave birth, I was amazed at how calm and collected the staff were with the whole frightening ordeal. They were obviously all too familiar with these unrestrained groans.

We in the church, on the other hand, being unfamiliar with any such desperation, are prone to hush the groans. Even with our initiations into the kingdom—our spiritual birthings, so to speak, the experience has become quite clinical.

Quietly raise a finger, repeat these words under your breath or in your mind if you wish, and slip into the new world of great benefits. No need to make too much noise—you'll wake the slumbering.

Our attitude is vastly different from Paul's or Peter's or any of the early Christians at large. We do not groan with eager expectation, because our expectation has fallen asleep. We do not wait breathlessly for the day of our salvation, because we have it already and are too busy trying to figure out how to put it to our advantage.

One has to wonder if we truly understand the good news at all. Buildings and programs and attendance and well-run services aren't the gospel, yet they preoccupy our minds. The fact that because of Christ there is coming a blessed day when we will finally be able to dive into God himself rather than be eternally separated from him, is the good news. We ought to let that reality ravage our minds.

The Race

One of the most interesting analogies used in the Bible to describe our lives is the analogy of a race. The writer of Hebrews compared our lives to that of a marathon runner, straining for the prize ahead. Read the passage that urges us to run the race with our eyes fixed on Jesus, who is our example and who ran his race for the joy set before him: heaven (12:1–2).

We know the passage well, but many tend to attribute the goal as being Jesus here and now, rather than following Christ in running the race for what lies ahead, the joy or bliss that awaits at the right hand of God.

But there is more to this brilliant word picture. Consider the marathons you may have watched over the years. Perhaps you've watched portions of the Olympic marathon. Who among the runners at the Olympics trains for many months and runs long, exhausting miles without thoughts of crossing the finish line, surrounded by a great cloud of witnesses cheering?

Who among the runners of any such race train and strain for anything less than the finish line?

Who among runners endure such punishment to the body for a lesser prize than finishing or winning the race?

Who runs the race for the cups of water along the way?

Yet we in the church seem more enamored by the water on our way to the finish line than by the finish line itself. We have lost our way and have gone chasing after the cupbearers who promise a sip of refreshing water, when the finish line awaits with its prize unclaimed.

> Who among the runners of any such race train and strain for anything less than the finish line? Who runs the race for the cups of water along the way? Yet many Christians have left the race and gone chasing after the cupbearers.

Are we to deny the water of the Spirit who has come to comfort our race? Of course not!

But we must never take our eyes off the joy set before us. We must fix our eyes on that prize—Christ in eternity. The race is not about the water along the way, but the prize at the end.

The Virgins' Lamps

At the end of his ministry, Jesus gave a provocative picture of the church in our day through a story about the end times. The tale is about ten virgins, or bridesmaids, who have prepared themselves for the wedding celebration, a foreshadowing of heaven. It starts out like this:

> At that time the kingdom of heaven will be like ten virgins who took their lamps and went out to meet the bridegroom. (Matt. 25:1)

Now, I don't know if you are engaged now, or ever have been, or hope to be one day, but I can assure you, a bride-to-be is a unique kind of person, whose infectious expectation and happiness spread to the bridesmaids, who care for her up to the moment of the wedding.

My wife has coordinated many weddings, and I am always amazed at the sheer volume of preparation and energy they consume. Why all the preparation, I ask, if the wedding is going to last only an hour or so and then be over? Why not just tie the knot and be done with it?

The answer is simple. Hope. The bride has in her mind an incredible and inexpressible hope for her marriage. The ceremony symbolically represents that hope or dream.

So the bride and her party purchase beautiful gowns and then lavishly decorate a hall and buy mounds of food that the bride and bridegroom will hardly touch because of their own excitement. The anticipation of a wedding is so strong that it will preoccupy the bride for months, giving her more pleasure than anyone who has never been a bride can possibly understand.

Throughout Scripture the wedding is repeatedly used as a metaphor for the day when the church will be united with Christ, and the wedding feast is symbolic of the celebration that heavenbound believers anticipate.

Jesus used the same metaphor here, but he expanded it to include a lamp with oil. There have been many interpretations of this oil, but I can't help thinking the oil must at least in part represent the same "oil" a bride brings to her own wedding. Namely, hope, that fruit of the Spirit oil so often symbolizes.

A burning hope.

Now let's see what happened:

Five of them were foolish and five were wise. The foolish ones took their lamps but did not take any oil with them. The wise, however, took oil in jars along with their lamps.

The bridegroom was a long time in coming, and they all became drowsy and fell asleep.

At midnight the cry rang out: "Here's the bridegroom! Come out to meet him!"

Then all the virgins woke up and trimmed their lamps. The foolish ones said to the wise, "Give us some of your oil; our lamps are going out."

"No," they replied, "there may not be enough for both us and you. Instead, go to those who sell oil and buy some for yourselves."

But while they were on their way to buy the oil, the bridegroom arrived. The virgins who were ready went in with him to the wedding banquet. And the door was shut.

Later the others also came. "Sir! Sir!" they said. "Open the door for us!"

But he replied, "I tell you the truth, I don't know you."

Therefore keep watch, because you do not know the day or the hour. (vv. 2–13)

This story is often referenced as a parable that shows we don't know when Christ will return. Yes, but there is much more here. There are those two words that scream out to us. *Keep watch*, because you do not know the day or the hour.

What does "keep watch" mean in the story? Which virgins kept watch? They all had slipped into a slumber, much the same as Christianity has slipped into a slumber today. Indeed, we all lose focus and drift off from time to time, even those of us with ample reserves of oil.

The only difference between the two sets of virgins was the

amount of oil they had brought with them. The wise and the foolish differed only in the amount of preparation their antici-pation of the wedding had fueled. And if oil represents hope for that day, then the only difference was in their hope.

They all had responded to the call, dressed for the occasion, lit their lamps, then fallen asleep. They all were awakened. But only five had the oil of hope to fuel their fires and light their way into the wedding feast.

Here is the critical rub. Only five had put enough fore-thought into the wedding feast to properly prepare. The rest had prepared, but their preparation appeared to have been halfhearted. They grabbed their lamps with what oil remained in the bowls and headed out.

The five wise virgins, however, applied themselves to a kind of preparation that protected them from weakening resolve—From running out of oil. Their determination to reach the wed-ding feast seems to have been greater than the others'.

Consider the parable at length and you will agree, the amount of oil carried by each virgin is the only tangible difference between them. Jesus fashioned an entire parable to illuminate this for us. This story seems to suggest that for those who have responded to the wedding feast invitation, the preparation will make some kind of difference in their journey.

The notion that we have some responsibility to secure oil for our journey to the wedding feast is an unpopular notion in Christianity today. Our religion is focused on quick fixes that require nothing. But here Jesus is clearly making the case that the virgins' responsibility to secure oil before the wedding was critical to their journey.

The Oil of Hope

In light of this parable, we must ask ourselves yet again, How deep are our reservoirs of hope? An interesting thing about hope, which we will see in the second half of this book, is that you can't snap your fingers and have it. You can't borrow it from your neighbor. It is a precious oil, pressed from the nuts and seeds that contain it. Don't think you'll be able to dip into a vast reservoir of oil when persecution comes or the trumpet calls. You must begin to coax it from the seeds of grace planted in your heart now, while there is still time.

Hope is something that lives in our hearts and minds and imaginations, not in what we already have now. Hope in what we already have, as Paul said, is no hope at all.

The oil of hope is one of the fruits of the Holy Spirit, deposited in us as a down payment on our own inheritance. Such a gift is undoubtedly one of God's greatest gifts to mankind.

And of all the gifts, hope is perhaps the most personal. You can show love, you can demonstrate faith, but you either *have* or *do not have* hope. The amount of hope you have, like oil, may be shown in how bright your lamp shines. You may attend a church filled with colorfully dressed Christians who sing and wave their lamps in celebration. But check the flames that light the path to the wedding feast, and you will know if the bridesmaids you dance with are wise or foolish.

The New Testament is like a seed itself, rich in the oil of hope. You can't read a single book without being soaked in it. The early church thrived on this oil. Hope lit their lamps and attracted thousands into a persecuted movement.

The early Christians eagerly awaited their inheritance. Each day they sang songs about death being swallowed up in victory at the end of days. Their entire faith burned with hope for a day that would soon come, not only for the days that had come.

It is time that we understand the true nature of our own faith. Christianity is as much about death as life. It's about the end of spiritual death, through a spiritual birth, made possible by Christ's death and resurrection. Death has become life, in part now, and in whole after this life. After we die.

And the way we engage this entire truth is through a small portal into the reality that lies beyond. The portal is hope.

But our eyes of hope have grown heavy and dark, and we can no longer see past the skin of this world into the next.

Answering Your Questions

We've covered a lot of relatively new ground for many readers, and we've done it in a fairly short presentation. Whenever you write on a subject that questions the status quo, there are bound to be many who wrestle with the issues. In the interest of clarifying, I would like to answer a few questions that might have surfaced.

I can't hope to be exhaustive in this short book. However, a brief look at the most common questions that I receive on the issues presented thus far might prove helpful for those who are still grappling with the slumber of Christianity.

> *Daily living in our world requires some level of concentration and hope in one's immediate future on this earth. There has to be some satisfaction found in "seizing the day." What is the ideal balance between living for today and living for the afterlife?*

You don't have to balance living for today and living for the afterlife. These two hopes are not in conflict. We don't live on a seesaw of hope where the hope of this life goes down if the hope for the afterlife goes up. In reality, they both go up and down together.

This is critical to understand. While it's true that you can have great hope for something in the next few days without having any hope for the afterlife, you can't have great hope for the afterlife and consequently lose hope for the next few days. Hope doesn't work that way. When you are confronted with a true hope for something down the road, the entire journey to that hope is brightened. To fall back on a familiar analogy, the journey to a wedding feast is brightened by the hope for that wedding feast.

Hope in the afterlife doesn't erase disappointments in this life, but it does cast them in a new light—a brighter, more hopeful light. As such, the hope written about in the New Testament is a no-lose proposition. No balance required. Indulge yourself on the hope of Christ for heaven and you'll find all your hopes in this life brightened.

> *Isn't it true that the state of experiencing an actual "yearning" for death or an afterlife would most likely be found in the elderly, the terminally ill, and the morbidly depressed? If given the opportunity, how many healthy, happy people would choose to be instantly transported from this earth to be with Christ?*

Now we come to the heart of the matter. How many would choose to be instantly transported to be with Christ, you ask? Very few, I say. Why, you ask? Because the slumber of Christianity has deadened the reality of heaven's bliss in the hearts and minds of most Christians.

Who in their right mind would choose the crumbs from the table of God when presented with the opportunity to feast at his table? Only those who think the crumbs *are* the feast, or those who've never truly desired the feast because they don't believe it to be a tangible, intoxicating reality.

The elderly often realize that the crumbs can't satisfy, although many are so used to eating crumbs that they, too, are in slumber.

I would say that "healthy, happy people," who would choose to stay here if confronted by a choice to be with Christ, are not nearly as healthy as they think they are. They simply can't know what they are missing. They are deadened to the great health and happiness that awaits. They are happy now only to the extent that eating crumbs can make those who don't know any better.

> **Wouldn't "craving to die and be with Christ" more appropriately be stated "craving to be with Christ when we die"?**

Characterizing the desire for heaven as something that should wait until you've exhausted the joys of this life undermines the value of being with Christ in a subtle yet crippling way.

I believe this is in part what Christ had in mind when he stated that anyone who did not hate his life (and family) could not be his disciple (Luke 14:26). His point is one of comparison. According to this teaching, if your passion for being with Christ isn't greater by far than remaining in this life (as Paul characterized his desire for heaven), then your motive for following Christ is suspicious (according to Christ).

We find a similar sentiment from our Lord when a disciple who wanted to follow him asked if he could first go and bury his father. "Let the dead bury the dead," Christ said (Matt. 8:22).

In both passages Christ is making the strong statement that being with him reduces the common expressions of love in this life (like burials) to trivial pursuits. The stuff of redemption and heaven is greater by far than anything this life has to offer.

Yet so many Christians have devalued heaven by seemingly reasonable statements, such as the one in the question above. "Surely," we say to ourselves, "craving to be with Christ when we die gives us the opportunity to enjoy both lives as God intended." Perhaps, but it also places too much value on this life and quickly leads to the death of passion for the next life.

> *How can anyone be certain that he or she is now truly "awake" and won't return to slumber?*

Do you have a deep desire to be with Christ today? Then you are awake. You can be as certain of never returning to slumber as you can of never sinning again. that the bottom line is, you *can't* be certain, and you must therefore guard your passion for Christ in the same way that five of the ten virgins guarded themselves against running out of oil for the coming wedding feast in Jesus' parable.

> *Do you believe that parents should not shield their children from violence in the media and entertainment?*

Certainly parents, myself included, do and must shield their children from excessive violence, wherever it presents itself. But we should never turn away from the leper for the sake of our own comfort. We should never ignore the brutality of the Cross so that we don't have to participate in the suffering of Christ.

We should never pretend violence doesn't affect our world because we are afraid to face the truth: that evil is a destructive force that has ravaged mankind. I do think that some Christians would rather pretend that evil doesn't exist than fight it. I've found that they tend to be people who have fashioned false walls around themselves for the sake of comfort. Unfortunately these same walls tend to isolate them from a real world in desperate need of a Savior.

Having said that, we should all be very careful not to expose ourselves or our children to any kind of evil that might undermine their passion and/or faith in God.

7

Created to Obsess

The Emotions of God

I recently had some rather extensive dental work done, and I found the experience quite unusual. Nitrous oxide, it turns out, deprives the brain of oxygen and acts as a mild anesthetic. Although my body wasn't sleeping, my mind very nearly was, and two hours seemed more like twenty minutes. It was almost as if I had been robbed of a chunk of my time. I had little understanding of what was being done to me in this oxygen-deprived state.

My brain was made for more oxygen than it was receiving. Within a few moments of returning the correct mixture of oxygen to my system, I awoke and the numbing effects of oxygen deprivation faded.

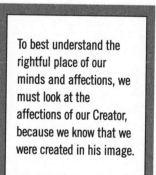

To best understand the rightful place of our minds and affections, we must look at the affections of our Creator, because we know that we were created in his image.

In the same way, the slumber to the truth of our inexhaustible inheritance can be awakened by returning our minds and affections to their rightful place.

To best understand the rightful place of our minds and affections, we must look at the affections of our Creator, because we know that we were created in his image (Gen. 1:27). This isn't to say that he made us with two arms and two legs and one nose because he had the same, but that we were fashioned in the image of his Spirit and his mind and his heart.

And the image of his emotions.

I am continually amazed at the dogged attempt by some Christians to minimize the emotions of man. Or worse, to secularize them as functions of the fallen human, divorced from the purity of God. But this is sacrilege. Don't emotions come from God? More to the point, doesn't God express emotion?

The fact is, throughout recorded history we have examples of God's expressing every imaginable emotion, from rage to joy, from profound sorrow to delight. Jesus wept at the death of Lazarus; Jesus raged through the temple with a whip; Jesus walked the earth filled with compassion.

Anger itself, then, if expressed by God himself, cannot possibly be considered evil. Inappropriate anger comes from the fallen nature, but we should be careful not to cut man off from emotions that are stamped on us by God.

Mice may not leap for joy when they find a morsel to eat, but we humans, created in the image of God, are entirely in character when we scream with delight. Worms may not weep when their cousins are plucked to be hooked for bait, but our own sorrow at death is understandable.

> Mice may not leap for joy when they find a morsel to eat, but we humans, created in the image of God, are entirely in character when we scream with delight.

Again, I appeal to the quote from C.S. Lewis that I introduced in chapter 1:

Indeed if we consider the unblushing promises of reward and the staggering nature of the rewards promised in the gospels, it would seem that our Lord finds our desires not

too strong, but too weak. We are halfhearted creatures . . .
We are far too easily pleased.

Hope, the Greatest Emotion

Think of the suppression of emotion as a terrible trick played on us by the enemy. Knowing that our faith is dependent in part on our hope (faith is the substance of things hoped for), the enemy has sought to condemn all emotion, intending to condemn hope with the rest. And in many quarters he's succeeded spectacularly.

Let's go back to *The American Heritage Dictionary*'s definition of *hope*: (1) to wish for something with expectation of its fulfillment (2) to look forward to something with confidence or expectation (3) to expect and desire. Hope is a desire. It is anticipation. It is an emotion, based on a positive expectation of something we believe will happen.

If you stand before a firing squad waiting to be shot, you have no hope, but only expectation. If you stand as a competitor in front of judges who are selecting the next national winner of some contest, you have hope, not simply expectation. The difference? Desire. Emotion.

If we don't abandon ourselves to hope for the afterlife, we certainly won't groan for it. If we discard hope as an untrustworthy emotion, or limit our hope to things that are immediately tangible, how can we develop great passion for something as intangible as heaven?

We can't.

And so it is no wonder that our hope for glory has been put to sleep. We are far more comfortable clinging to and hoping for what we can see, here in this life, than hoping in a future that is not yet seen. As a result we have directed our hope toward objectives that are immediately tangible, the *foretastes* of the bliss that awaits us, and away from that which awaits us itself.

Treasure

Let me tell you a story. There once was a wealthy man named John Caldwell who owned a large spread of land in Colorado just north of the San Juan Mountains. Next to his land there was a small parcel owned by Cecil Riggens, an old codger who lived in a twenty-foot log cabin. John and Cecil knew each other, but you wouldn't call them friends.

One day John was replacing a rotted fence post on his boundary line when he noticed what he thought was water wetting his neighbor's land. He slipped under the fence and walked toward the large dark splotch.

But it wasn't water. John had gained his wealth during the oil boom in Texas, and he knew the moment he touched the dirt that he was kneeling over a rich oil reservoir. Rarely did oil find its way so near the surface, particularly in Colorado. The details that came out in the lawsuit several years later amounted to this:

For a week, John considered telling the old codger about the oil on his land, but the more he thought about it, the more he began to realize just how much wealth this oil reserve could produce. He slipped onto Cecil's land at night and took samples and when those samples came back, his suspicions were confirmed. The land his neighbor sat on was worth a mint.

John began to develop an obsession. His own wealth, though not depleted, was a fraction of his neighbor's. A month went by, and by this time, John could think of nothing but that plot of land next to his. Late one night he finally decided on a course of action he hoped might work.

The next morning John went to Cecil and explained that he had to file bankruptcy due to some bad business dealings. His own net worth was too much for the IRS to ignore, so he had a plan that would make Cecil rich. He proposed an even trade—Cecil's land for his land.

After recovering from his shock at being offered such a lucrative deal, Cecil agreed and the properties were exchanged.

Three months later an oil well went up. Another three months, and Cecil filed a lawsuit.

John won the lawsuit. End of story.

You recognize the tale, don't you? Of course you do. I've embellished it and I've changed the setting, but for the most part you've just read a version of a story Jesus told two thousand years ago. His version was shorter and went like this:

> The kingdom of heaven is like treasure hidden in a field. When a man found it, he hid it again, and then in his joy went and sold all he had and bought that field. (Matt. 13:44)

My version highlights a particular aspect of this story that most Christians overlook. The field the man found the treasure in wasn't *his*. It belonged to someone else. Didn't this man have a moral obligation to inform the lawful owner that he sat on a veritable mint? Instead, our protagonist rushed out and did something quite deceptive.

He didn't offer to buy the treasure from the true owner, but he bought the land, knowing that the owner didn't realize the true value of that land. If this part of the story wasn't important, Jesus could have simply stated that the man sold all he had (a statement of deep desire) and bought the treasure. But he didn't choose to tell the tale that way.

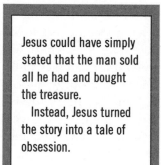

Jesus could have simply stated that the man sold all he had and bought the treasure.

Instead, Jesus turned the story into a tale of obsession.

Instead, Jesus turned the story into a tale of *obsession*.

I realize that I've chosen a strong word, but strong words are sometimes needed to wake the slumbering from deep sleep.

Think about it. What kind of man sells all he has to buy a field? A man obsessed with that field or, as in this case, the treasure in that field.

Clearly, Christ wasn't *promoting* deception, but he obviously thought it was a useful tool in showing just how far someone might go to secure the kingdom of heaven. He was promoting a kind of obsession with the kingdom of heaven.

Obsession

If there is one driving sentiment that heaven is worthy of, it is obsession. Unfortunately, like desire and passion, obsession has been dirtied by the world. Pure, irresistible desire has been undermined in many parts of the church. Yet it perhaps best characterizes the kind of hope the early church had for the bliss that awaited them after this life. Let's take a closer look at this word.

> *Obsession*: (1) a persistent disturbing preoccupation with an often unreasonable idea or feeling; *broadly*: compelling motivation. (*Webster's Collegiate Dictionary, 11th edition*)

The man from Jesus' parable of the treasure in the field was indeed compelled by a persistent preoccupation with a somewhat unreasonable idea, was he not? This is the missed point of the story. The man did something rather unorthodox to obtain something he obviously thought was unattainable any other way. He sold all he had, a tremendous sacrifice, and he went to great lengths to own the treasure by buying the field that contained it.

He was guided by his obsession. Foolish in the eyes of the law, yes, but his reward was indeed great. Our teacher's point isn't that we all should find deceptive ways to gain wealth. It is simply that the kingdom of heaven is like a treasure, and that treasure is worthy of our greatest obsession.

Surrounded by the Obsessed

I've seen plenty of obsessed Christians in my time. They are usually new to the faith, and they tend to bounce off the walls in their enthusiasm. Talk about cars with them and they'll find a way to turn the subject back to Christ. Talk about food and they will tell you they have lost their hunger for the things of this world.

They have a new compelling motivation. They have a persistent preoccupation with an unreasonable feeling. They are obsessed.

Have no fear, new Christian. You are in good historical company.

- *John the Baptist* was obsessed. His obsession with a simple message—prepare your hearts for the coming Messiah—compelled him to live in the desert, wear gunnysacks, and eat insects. He was thoroughly preoccupied by an unreasonable idea.

- *David* was obsessed. His whole life reads like a maniac's, so passionate was he for his Deliverer. Yet he was the one man in history called out by God as having a heart most like God's.

- *Paul* was obsessed. He spent years alone in the desert, feeding on the Spirit's revelation, before throwing himself into a dogged determination to spread the light to the lost. Through it all he considered dying to be with Christ far better than living on earth.

The list of obsessed men and women of faith could easily fill this book and then some. History is made by obsessed humans who are captivated by a compelling motivation for something they do not yet have. That would be heaven for the Christian. Complete happiness. Bliss.

Question: Is God obsessed?

If you say no, either you haven't read his story or you've not understood it. The only difference between his compelling motivation to live as a human and die on the cross and our own motivation is that his required no faith. But his passion far exceeded any we are even capable of in this life.

God is obsessive. Remember *Webster's* definition of *obsession*? God is indeed driven by a compelling motivation, a persistent preoccupation with an idea that is beyond our ability to reason. His ways confound the wise, and his passion for you is beyond understanding.

He is preoccupied with you. He is determined to save you from his own wrath. He has wiped out many cities to protect his own. He destroyed the earth with a flood in his anguish. He goes to unthinkable lengths to find those who will allow him to love them. And in the end he will once again destroy the earth in the most spectacular fashion for the sake of his kingdom.

Because his ways are beyond our understanding, many people discount the records of what he has done as a fairy tale. Many humans dismiss even the *idea* of God because he makes no sense to them.

Yes, God is obsessive. Many frown on that term, but our faith in part depends on it. God is obsessed, and now we, too, can be obsessed.

We can preoccupy our minds with an unreasonable treasure and enamor our hearts with the hope of glory.

Heaven, a Treasure Worthy of Our Obsession

At this point there are still those who may object to my characterization of the treasure in Christ's parable. Their minds are so firmly planted in this life that they still insist our treasure, the kingdom of heaven, is here on earth. Now.

Yes, the treasure is here now, but only as a foretaste of the great bliss that awaits us. We do have incomparably great power to live victorious lives as we await our salvation, but we must understand that this power is designed to propel us down the road to our destiny. Heaven. That is the goal we are running for. And the moment we take our eyes off that prize, our power to run the race to the finish is compromised.

> The incomparable great power we have as believers is tied up in hope. Lose the hope and lose the power.

The incomparable great power we have as believers is tied up in hope. Lose the hope and lose the power.

Consider the use of the word *treasure* elsewhere in the New Testament. Jesus said:

> Provide purses for yourselves that will not wear out, a treasure *in heaven* that will not be exhausted, where no thief comes near and no moth destroys. For where your treasure is, there your heart will be also. (Luke 12:33–34, emphasis added)

And Paul said:

> In this way they [those who put their hope in God (v.17)] will lay up treasure for themselves as a firm foundation for the *coming age*, so that they may take hold of the life that is truly life. (1 Tim. 6:19, emphasis added)

What bold statements! Where your treasure is, there your heart *will be* also. If the treasure you obsess after is on this earth, your heart will remain on this earth; but if your treasure is in heaven, your heart will be there as well.

Life that is truly life, Paul said, is a life fixated on the coming age.

Let me ask you, where is the church's treasure today? Is it in the earthly benefits of Christianity, these wonderful gifts of wealth and food and clothing bestowed on us by our Father? Or is our treasure in the age to come, in heaven, where it cannot be spoiled and where life is truly life?

We can answer this question by asking where most Christians' hearts are. Where are their passions and desires and hopes? Talk about the bliss of glory, and you get a dull stare. Talk about a vacation to the Caribbean, and you see the glint of hope in the slumberer's eyes.

Don't look at your neighbor's eyes; look in a mirror. Walk up to that mirror and say, "Heaven." Do your eyes light up?

I've tried not to belabor this point of obsession, because I find it nearly self-evident, and I'm assuming that by informing you just a little, you have quickly agreed with me. If not, read Job, a great passion play between obsessive players. Read David's story and songs. Read of Paul's journeys. Read John's revelation. Read Jeremiah and Isaiah and Ezekiel. Read about Jonah and Cain and Elijah and Esther and Noah. Stories of men and women consumed by a vision of God, driven by a compelling motivation and a persistent preoccupation with an often unreasonable idea. Stories of obsession.

Obsession and Reason

Here's a simple question: Is Christianity, as a religion, reasonable?

One would have to say yes. It has its social benefits. It fills a need for understanding in the same way that all religions do. We have our traditions and our services and our faith, and these all help make the world a happier place in which to live. Christianity is reasonable.

But is following Christ reasonable?

This is where the paths of Christianity as a religion and following Christ part ways in dramatic fashion. The fact is, following Christ is not a very reasonable thing to do in the eyes of unbelievers. Our following is based on faith, not on reason. There's a tremendous amount of reason along the way, yes, but the journey itself is based on faith. This is a critical distinction when it comes to understanding hope.

We in the West are obsessed with reason, in the same way that I am going to suggest we be obsessed with hope. Our preoccupation with reason is what leads us to conclude that emotion is untrustworthy after we see it failing us repeatedly. So it could be said that one of the casualties of our reason is emotion, or passion for the afterlife. Our slumber is, in part, brought on by reason.

Despite my collegiate studies in philosophy, I would argue that we ought to embrace the unreasonableness of our faith. The *hope* we have—which I have argued is based on emotion, not reason—results in our groaning for heaven. Yes, evidence demands our verdict, but as we will soon see, the faith described in the New Testament springs out of hope, the emotion behind faith.

> Yes, evidence demands our verdict, but as we will soon see, the faith described in the New Testament springs out of hope, the emotion behind faith.

As a storyteller, I read dozens of film reviews because I'm curious about what the self-appointed critics across the country are saying about these mainstream stories that shape culture. When *The Passion of the Christ* outstripped everyone's wildest expectations at the box office, the mainstream media was flummoxed. Not only confused, but disturbed. Outraged! There was one question on all of their lips: *How could such a brutal, nonsensical slaughter inspire so many people? What was there to follow here? Christianity is about loving your neighbor and making peace with governments and feeding the poor, not this bloody mess on the screen.*

It is at moments like this when the vast gulf between those who have been saved by Christ's senseless slaughter and those who have not comes into brilliant focus. True faith in Christ not only draws inspiration from his death, but is *based* on that brutal, ugly, bloody, beautiful, and, yes, to the world, senseless death.

What's more, we Christians claim to live a life of death that brings life. "Take up your cross and follow me," Christ called. We are now dead to sin, buried and risen with Christ. True, Christianity hinges on the resurrection of Christ, and we like to live in resurrection power, but resurrection comes only after death and will not be complete until the day of our salvation after Christ returns.

In the meantime, we take up our crosses daily.

None of this talk of death makes a lick of sense to people outside the faith. Even Christians tend to shove it into a dark corner, because on the surface it seems to undermine the gospel of great benefits that the church is so preoccupied with.

Consider our sacraments. Christ asked his followers to follow two rituals after his death. Communion, a ritual in which the participant pretends to drink Christ's blood and eat his body in memory of his sacrifice. And baptism, a ritual in which the participant symbolically dies and is buried and then rises again, a new creature.

The world sees these sacraments, but it doesn't understand them, certainly not as for civilized man. Today many in the church feel uncomfortable with them as well. The sacraments aren't entirely reasonable. They are actually quite unreasonable. The whole *rose again, born again, drink his blood, go to paradise* thing just doesn't make a lot of sense to most non-Christians.

But is the gospel supposed to make sense? Not to those who don't have faith. Paul said: "The message of the cross is foolishness to those who are perishing, but to us who are being saved it is the power of God" (1 Cor. 1:18).

Let me restate. The gospel is unreasonable to those who do not follow Christ, but for those of us who are in the process of being saved from God's wrath at the end of time, the message of the Cross is power!

But what if we who are *being* saved take our eyes off the great message of redemption at the end of time? Then we place responsibility for all of the gospel's benefits on this life, and when those benefits fail to materialize as we once hoped they would, the gospel begins to sound a little foolish to us as well.

It is critical that we step back and see our faith for what it is: a profound commitment to something we *hope* for, not a faith based on reason. Our faith is based more on emotion than on reason.

Paul made the point clear: faith springs from hope, not from fact or reason (Col. 1:5). Faith is the substance of things *hoped* for, not the substance of things proven (Heb. 11:1). Paul's faith came from a knowledge informed by his hope and experience. The great apostle hinged his faith on a desire.

> It is critical that we step back and see our faith for what it is: a profound commitment to something we *hope* for, not a faith based on reason. Our faith is based more on emotion than on reason.

The day I tried to prove my faith in college was the day I lost that faith. When we shift the focus of our faith from the eyes of the heart to a purely rational exploration of fact, our faith will almost certainly weaken.

We may still believe, but we are far less likely to become like children consumed with a simple faith. And we are surely less likely to become like a child obsessed with a fast-approaching Christmas.

Should we kill reason, then? No! We will always depend on reason, because we were created as reasoning beings.

But we must not allow reason to kill our obsession for the afterlife. We must not sacrifice an obsession for that which we don't yet see with an obsession for pleasures in this life.

The *fact—faith—feeling* train we've all grown up with has its merits. In this model, fact accepted by faith drives the trains of our lives, and the small caboose of feeling trails along help-lessly in tow.

But according to Hebrews, faith is being sure of what we *hope* for, not of a set of facts that lead our lives. The engine of our lives is more hope than fact, regardless of what we may have been taught. Birds and butterflies live in a world guided solely by the set of facts that surround them. They perform various functions based on a strict set of requirements for life.

Not we humans, created in the image of God. We are guided by desire. We were created to hope, and the greatest kind of hope is nothing less than a form of obsession.

The Sum of the Matter

The sum of the matter is this: We humans are naturally obses-sive creatures. We tend to fixate on objectives and dreams, and we are quite good at achieving whatever our minds conceive. Why is this? Because we were created in the image of a God who has a similar nature. His ways are beyond our under-standing because they aren't bound by human reasoning and his obsession is not an entirely rational thing.

We were designed to obsess after our Creator. But our hearts have been corrupted, and the agent of evil, Satan himself, has successfully redirected our obsession away from God, and his great reward for all those who love him, by fill-ing our minds solely with things of this earth.

Being creatures created to obsess, many have redirected their obsession to the pleasures of this world alone.

Christians have fallen asleep to the promise of the afterlife and no longer dream of that great day. Their obsession for eternity is in slumber. And being creatures created to obsess, many have redirected their obsession to the pleasures of this world alone.

Confronted by a flock following hard after the world, many teachers in the church have tended to denounce obsession altogether rather than reawaken a passion for the coming bliss. Why? Because they, too, have lost their own desperate longing for that day.

But I say with Paul, fix your mind on heaven. Fascinate your mind with Christ, and fan into flames a vision of the afterlife.

Obsess after the bliss that awaits you as a joint heir with Christ in heaven.

But how? you ask. You've tried and feel no obsession for the afterlife. How do you fascinate your mind with eternity, of all things? How do you awaken a passion for the next life while living in this life?

Surely it's not as simple as flipping a switch somewhere and waking from a deep slumber. Surely it's not a matter of gritting your teeth and trying harder.

Awakening to passion for heaven on earth begins by exposing the slumber that has stolen that passion and understanding the critical role the emotion of hope plays in any passion for the bliss to come. This we have done.

Now let's see how we might further awaken hope.

PART II

Shaking Off Our Slumber

8

The Eyes of the Heart

Unveiling True Pleasure

Good news!

I heard while on a trip to Atlanta a few days ago that the bladder test came back negative. No cancer cells found in the surrounding fluid. This means I have four more weeks before they do another test to find out what's happening inside me.

The thought of that test sends chills down my spine. My body wasn't created for such tests.

I wonder what my response would have been if the test had come back positive? I think I would have found immediate peace for myself. A trip to the heavens is a rather intoxicating prospect when you consider it in the light of that great adventure set before us. But would it have changed the way I live, short of any physical limitations? What does it matter if we are to die in ten years or ten months?

My wife and children . . . I don't know how I would have responded to the prospect of my wife and children living on without me. If, in C. S. Lewis's terms, I were to depart for the holiday by the sea sooner than they, would they manage? Would they be angry? Would they be jealous? It would all depend on their perspective of heaven, deep down inside where no one else really knows.

Before the end of the book, four weeks will have passed, and I will tell you what happens in this continuing saga of mine. In the meantime, we must learn how to awaken from a slumber that has deadened our desperate desire for heaven.

We must awaken a passion for heaven on earth.

The Dark Room

I've characterized hope as a pearl of great price that can be placed in the heart to bring the machine of happiness roaring to life. There is another way to look at hope. A short analogy:

There is a dark cellar. The walls of this cellar are a bit of a mystery to you. They represent all that is good and evil. Although you can barely see them, you begin to make out their basic construction.

There are smooth stones that awe you and rough stones that cut your fingers. Water drips somewhere—you can hear it but you can't see it. Small animals scurry about, which is frightening, but you can't see to deal with them, so you stay clear of their pattering. It's cold and damp.

The room also has chairs and a table filled with food, barely visible in the dim light. There are some paintings on the walls—you can feel them but can't make out their colors. The room both fascinates you and frustrates you.

This is your life.

You're not quite sure what to make of it. At times the room fills you with mystery. Your initial discovery of the room feels quite adventurous. Some of the food is quite good, and even though much of it is moldy and you have a hard time picking out the good pieces from the bad, you overlook the bitter tastes and dig out another piece. The only light and warmth come from a tiny lamp on one wall.

But as you grow older in this dark, cold place, you begin to tire of the food, and the darkness begins to suffocate you. The bitter foods begin to take their toll, and in your exploring of the walls, the rough stones cut your hands. The room begins to feel like a prison. There is no way out. In fact, it never occurs to you that anything exists beyond the room.

Eventually, you become hopeless and settle for living out your days in the dark. This is best done by sleeping, so you slip into a slumber.

Then one day a brick falls out from the wall high above your head, and a bright shaft of light streams into the room. You jump back in awe, stunned by the brilliance. After you recover from the shock, you stand on the table and pass your hand through the shaft and feel a new warmth. Some of the walls around you are now clearly visible, and for the first time you see true color. You also see the rough stones to avoid and the spoiled food to push away.

But it's the light that draws your attention more than what that light reveals. There's more to life than this room; you know that now. If only you could escape from the room and break into the light that beckons you. Unfortunately, the hole in the wall is large enough for only your arm, and you can't seem to dislodge any more of the wall.

For weeks you sit in the light's warmth and stare at the white hole, dreaming of what lies beyond. You're grateful that you now can see more of the room, and you take advantage of its illumination.

But soon you begin to take the hole for granted, and you eventually forget that it leads anywhere. Over time the hopelessness you once felt returns, and you again settle for living out your days in a dim room. Once again you find that slumber is the better way to spend those days.

Welcome to the prison of our own making that we have studied thus far. The light is the bright light of hope that has lost its power to quicken our passion for life beyond this world.

But this analogy falls short, because now we must learn how to see beyond the four dark walls that dim our world. Now we will learn how to open our eyes from the slumber that has deadened our hopes. And now we will begin to use new words to describe this most critical element of our faith.

The Eyes of the Heart

Most Christians speak as though their spiritual beings are far more material than their bodies, yet they tend to dismiss spiritualism for fear of heresy prompted primarily by the New Age movement. We say we fight against principalities and powers and our pleasure is of another world, but we stay firmly planted in this world, concerning ourselves with the walls that hold us prisoner and the food at our dimly lit tables.

If we are primarily spiritual beings, we should concern ourselves with spiritual discovery. And this is no cause for worry, because our Creator has well equipped us for that primary discovery.

There has been much talk over time about the difference between the soul, the spirit, and the body. We don't need to launch into yet one more dissection of these terms. In keeping with the advice I've given my children to focus their theology on those doctrines that the New Testament writers made abundantly clear through repetition, we should focus on the most basic part of our beings most referenced by the same New Testament writers.

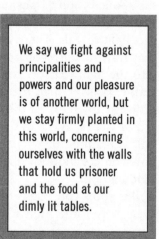

We say we fight against principalities and powers and our pleasure is of another world, but we stay firmly planted in this world, concerning ourselves with the walls that hold us prisoner and the food at our dimly lit tables.

The mind. And by mind, I mean all that is not physical about our bodies, including emotion. Although we speak of emotion as a heart condition, that pumping in our chests moves blood, not feelings. Emotions originate in our thinking, so for this book, let's keep them there.

Let me state clearly right up front that the mind is where hope resides, and it is through this window called hope that we most readily touch heaven.

I'm not talking about reason, mind you. We've discussed the limitations of pure reason and determined that it can fail to expand our understanding of what we cannot see with our eyes. But there is another kind of understanding available to the mind, and it is this understanding we should seek to illuminate.

Remember our primary definition of *hope*? To wish for something with expectation of its fulfillment. Is your left toe capable of wishing for a dream to come true? Do your eyes see a wish? Of course not.

Hope resides in the mind—in the heart, that place in the mind where emotion resides.

We desire the fulfillment of a dream or an outcome we have seen with our *minds*. We don't see the object of hope (in this case the bliss of the afterlife) with our physical eyes in a way that allows us to prove its existence. We see the bliss of heaven with the *eyes of our hearts*, so to speak, and when we see that bliss, we develop a great desire to attain it.

But what if we don't "see" the bliss of the afterlife? What if the idea of heaven is nothing more than a fuzzy picture without definition? Is it possible to have desire for something we don't even see or know?

No!

Hope, that gift God has given us to motivate our faith, is impossible to see if the eyes of your heart are closed.

If the eyes of the heart can't see heaven, the mind will never obsess after it. Most Christians have no vision at all of the afterlife, much less a vision of it that is attractive or inspiring. The eyes of their hearts have grown heavy and have subsequently been closed by slumber, and they no longer see the afterlife with the eyes of their hearts. Without a vision of heaven in clear view, they quickly lose interest.

But how does one *see* heaven to develop an obsession for it?

In our analogy of the dark room, how does the man trapped within its four walls develop a deep desire for what lies beyond the room unless he can first see what he's missing?

We have a view of heaven from two brilliant angles. The first is by way of a mirror called the pleasures of this life, which we will examine in the next chapter.

But there is another, perhaps more revealing, view of heaven available to all us creatures created in God's image.

It is the window called metaphor.

The eyes of the heart see with a vision that brings knowledge through metaphor and analogy and word pictures and story. It is a vision that resides in the mind and the heart, but it is no less spectacular than any vision seen with the eyes.

If we all were to visit heaven, as Paul himself did, or as John the apostle did, we might have no problem nurturing a brilliant, undying hope for it, because we tend to lean on our eyes more than our hearts or minds. But this in no way detracts from the way God intended most of us to *see* heaven now, while we are on earth.

A Prayer That Echoes Through History

In light of the early church's preoccupation with hope as articulated by the apostle Paul, and in light of this window into heaven through our minds and hearts, Paul's prayer for the Ephesians makes perfect sense:

> I pray also that the eyes of your heart may be enlightened in order that you may know the hope to which he has called you, the riches of his glorious inheritance in the saints, and his incomparably great power for us who believe. (Eph. 1:18–19)

Question: What did Paul mean by "the eyes of your heart"? He answers the question himself later in the same sentence when he describes the benefits of opening these eyes: "in order that you may *know* . . ."

Opening the eyes of the heart leads to knowledge. Knowledge as in *brain function* knowledge, not some esoteric fuzzy thing that leads us nowhere. There is no mystery to Paul's prayer. He wanted our minds to be opened so we could *know* something. Know what?

Hope!

The hope of what?

The hope of the glorious inheritance that awaits all believers.

But why did Paul use such an interesting phrase as "eyes of the heart" if he simply meant "mind"? Why didn't he just say, "I pray that your minds will be opened"?

Because he was leading up to a point about hope, and hope is a desire, something that is commonly attributed to the *heart*. So he wisely used this insightful phrase: "I pray also that the *eyes of your heart* may be enlightened."

Put another way he might have said, "I pray that the reasoning or understanding or the thoughts that inform your desires will be expanded so that your heart or emotions may grasp the hope of your inheritance."

Paul was praying that his readers' minds would be expanded so they might understand the richness of the bliss that awaited them in a way that fueled their desire. He was begging them to envision heaven. He was crying out for them to have a clear vision of their inheritance.

This is more than just a picture. It is a story that excites passion. An analogy that affects the heart. A vision of something not yet seen that ignites the imagination with fresh revelation.

A Theology of the Imagination

Like desire and obsession, imagination has been hijacked by the world. Again, no wonder, considering what a critical gift it is for Christians.

To say that connecting the imagination with hope is a new thing would overstate the case. Once again, consider the quote by C. S. Lewis from *The Weight of Glory*. He suggested that we in the church have far too weak desires for the rewards promised, because we don't understand those rewards:

> We are halfhearted creatures, fooling about with drink and sex and ambition when infinite joy is offered to us, like an ignorant child who wants to go on making mud pies in the slum because he cannot imagine what is meant by the offer of a holiday by the sea. We are far too easily pleased.

Like ignorant children, we can't *imagine* the holiday by the sea. And if our imagination of that holiday—that land of bliss—were to come alive? We would run to the sea and leave our mud pies behind, would we not?

Do birds use their imaginations? Do ants or worms? It is we humans, created in the image of God, who are blessed with an imagination. And it is through the imagination that our hope is primarily informed.

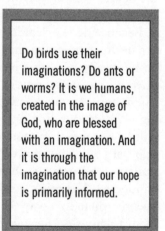

Do birds use their imaginations? Do ants or worms? It is we humans, created in the image of God, who are blessed with an imagination. And it is through the imagination that our hope is primarily informed.

What is the imagination? Let's start by demystifying this word. *Webster's* dictionary gives us a simple definition:

> The act or power of forming a mental image of something not present to the senses.

As humans, we use our imaginations without reprieve. All of our decisions are based on some kind of imagination. We imagine outcomes to given situations or actions, and we choose our responses or actions accordingly. Everything that is not immediately present to the senses is accessed by the imagination.

Example: If you place coffee and water in the appropriate receptacles in the coffeemaker, you will have freshly brewed coffee in about five minutes. The image of that fresh coffee is an imagination. You can't yet touch or taste or smell the coffee, because it is not yet *present to the senses*.

When the coffee is finished brewing and you pour yourself a cup, you imagine what it will taste like, and based on that imagination, you drink it.

If you think about this carefully, you will quickly discover that we live in a world of imagination. The moment something becomes reality, it passes into history, right? Our minds are occupied primarily with memories of the past and imaginations of what might occur later. We experience the present, but that experience is so fleeting that our primary engagement of any experience is through the imagination, either in the form of anticipation or memory. We depend on our imaginations.

So let's embrace imagination for a moment. It is a gift from our Creator.

Now let's define *imagination* again: An imagination is the God-breathed ability to consider *something* not perceived by our senses in the immediate reality.

Something like the inheritance we have awaiting us in heaven. Something like our Father's house, which has many rooms. Something like a bliss that would make Paul boldly proclaim that his dying to be with Christ would be better *by far* than living to serve him.

Our *hope* for the afterlife is informed by our perception of that afterlife, and that perception is something we imagine, full of confidence and faith.

Or, as is the case with most Christians, we don't imagine at all, and thus our hope for the afterlife is weak or nonexistent.

Listen to the way Dr. Eugene Peterson, author of *The Message*, makes this link between imagination and hope in his book *A Long Obedience*:

> Hoping is not dreaming. It is not spinning an illusion or fantasy to protect us from our boredom or our pain . . . It [hope] is imagination put in the harness of faith.

I realize these terms are not ordinary—and that is good, because we need a new paradigm to jolt us out of the slumber.

Again I will ask, are you desperate for heaven? No? May I suggest it's because you have no living hope for the bliss of heaven? And you have no living hope because you imagine heaven to be far less interesting than the earthly vacation you have your eyes on, or the man you would like to marry. Your imagination in regard to the vacation or the man is fully fleshed out. You've already picked out the destination for the vacation and the tuxedo for the man.

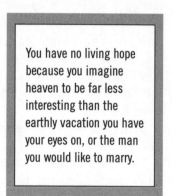

You have no living hope because you imagine heaven to be far less interesting than the earthly vacation you have your eyes on, or the man you would like to marry.

But your imagination of heaven might be flat. Lifeless. Boring.

The Good, the Bad, and the Beautiful

It goes without saying that, like desires and obsessions, there are good and bad imaginations. *Webster's* says that the imagination is a power, and indeed it is—a potent creative power that flows from heaven itself. But we fallen creatures have a way of turning good gifts into devices that kill.

Vain imagination and knowledge can put us into a self-destructive spiral, the Word tells us. These are the kind of imaginations we have run from. If we humans live most of our lives propelled by imagination, then clearly much of those imaginations are destructive, because much of our lives are filled with destructive behavior.

Using the same reasoning, on the other hand, all that is good in our behavior is motivated by good imagination.

One of the most obvious kinds of imagination is a thing we in the church like to call "vision." We do love our vision. This is our universally accepted good imagination, so I will use it to my advantage in making my point.

Vision drives our fund-raisers and builds our churches. It develops organizations and leads to wonderful ministries that cover the earth. I have no argument against any of these results.

Vision is a good thing.

But vision is nothing more, or less, than raw imagination. It is a perceived outcome that follows a plan of action with the hopes of achieving that outcome. *Envisioning* an outcome, such as heaven, is the same as *imagining* that outcome.

I love Bill Hybel's definition of *vision* in his book *Courageous Leadership*. "Vision," he says, "is a *picture* of the *future* that produces passion within us."

"I have a dream," Martin Luther King Jr. cried. "Not something that already is, but something that resides in my mind," he might have explained. All great things begin with this kind of imagined outcome we call vision. And without this kind of imagination, we become small, hopeless people who slip into a deep slumber.

I would say that although vain imaginations can be destructive, trying to live without a carefully formed imagination will necessarily lead to death. Consider the following teaching from the wisest man on earth, King Solomon:

Where there is no vision, the people perish. (Prov. 29:18 KJV)

Where there is no imagined outcome fueled by the creative power granted us by God, our hope will surely die and we will slip into a deep slumber.

And we have.

Our holy imaginations inform our hopes with more than blank or fuzzy thoughts that sit in our minds like dumb rocks. Hope then motivates our faith by quickening our anticipation for the object of our faith. And faith saves us from the wrath of God, for it is by grace through faith that we are saved. Do you see how critical our imaginations are? Our hope of the afterlife depends on them.

In fact, we experience God primarily through our imaginations.

Our experience of God is based on faith and hope, not on what we can see now, as Paul so emphatically insisted; otherwise, it would be no hope at all. So when I say that we experience God primarily through our imaginations, I am saying nothing new. I'm simply using rather pointed terms to say what we all already know. Our interaction with God occurs in our minds and hearts.

In our holy, God-given, beautiful imaginations.

Think and Feel and Hope for Heaven

I heard a most excellent sermon this week. I had traveled to a church, and the minister at the pulpit was speaking of the mind and about drawing strength from captive thoughts. I was pleasantly surprised when he quoted a verse I had intended to use in this very book, Colossians 3:2:

Set your minds on things above, not on earthly things.

The teacher of this good-sized church read the verse aloud, but before I could whisper a hearty "Amen," he followed his reading with a statement that made my stomach turn. "Paul's not talking about heaven," the well-intending man said, "but about the things of God."

I nearly choked, and to the best of my recollection I mumbled "Please," quietly enough not to be heard, I hope.

The fact of the matter is, Paul most certainly was talking precisely about heaven. The reason the teacher went out of his way to dismiss heaven as Paul's subject here was because he, like most of us, knew that most people are bored to tears with the notion of heaven. We have the misguided notion that talking about something as esoteric as heaven doesn't reward us now, and Christianity has become all about *now*.

Read the verse in context:

Since, then, you have been raised with Christ, set your hearts on things above, where Christ is seated at the right hand of God. (Col. 3:1)

Stop. Could Paul have been any clearer about what he meant by "above"? He drew a picture and that picture was of a place, not the "things of God." He began by urging us to set our hearts—our emotions—on heaven. Verses 2–4 say:

Set your minds on things above, not on earthly things. For you died, and your life is now hidden with Christ in God. When Christ, who is your life, appears, then you also will appear with him in glory.

This passage is yet one more treasure trove of support for my entire case. Much as he did in Ephesians, Paul included the heart as well as the mind—both critical elements in hope—when urging us to direct our lives toward the future reward, which he here described as appearing with Christ in glory.

Once again, Paul directed us to the future, not the present. The present is our death and resurrection with Christ. But the death and resurrection of Christ are fulfilled in what follows: our inheritance. Bliss eternal. This is something worth meditating on. This is what we ought to set our minds on. This is something worthy of our hearts' full passion.

We must understand that hope is an emotion, a desire that is fanned into flame by the mind. If our thinking is set on the pleasures of heaven, our hearts are far more likely to desire what we imagine.

Quickening the Imagination

Dr. Francis Shaeffer asked the question *How Should We Then Live?* Considering the slumber of Christianity, I think it would be appropriate to consider a more focused question: *How should we then imagine?*

How, then, should we set our minds on the things above? How, then, should we inform our minds with the riches of the bliss that awaits so that we can be empowered to follow Christ? Our hearts (emotions) guide us, but our emotions are fanned into flame by our understanding (minds). Therefore, we want to know how to fill our minds with something that will inflame our hearts toward the things of heaven.

We have been blessed with this wonderful thing called the imagination, and it is primarily through our imaginations that we see God. Through the eyes of the heart, where we imagine what we can't yet see and are drawn to it like a moth is drawn to the flame. Then with Paul we will be able to say, "For me, to die and be with Christ is better by far!"

God's Holy Word Pictures

This brings us back to envisioning or imagining heaven in the mind. There is one kind of literary device so heavily used in the Bible that many people unintentionally take it for granted. Figurative language. Metaphors and similes and other kinds of analogies.

Word pictures.

Many are familiar to all of us. Israel is like a whore who has left her lover to sleep with the enemy. God is the Lion of Judah. Christ is the Lamb of God. The Bible contains whole books filled with poetry, such as the Song of Solomon, in which nearly every word written is figurative. We have the Psalms, which lean on figurative lyrics in nearly every chapter.

We discover that the messages of the prophets are frequently delivered in figurative language. Isaiah, Ezekiel, and Jeremiah, among others, tell long and analogous tales that are figurative.

Then we have Revelation, apocalyptic literature that requires figurative language to communicate what will happen in the future.

God is infinitely intelligent, and since he is the one behind all this figurative language, we must assume that it was and is to this day one of the best ways, if not *the* best way, to communicate and understand truth.

But what is figurative language, except language that allows the reader to see a figure in his mind and imagine that the subject at hand is like that figure?

Are you hearing this? God leans heavily on the human imagination when communicating with humanity. In fact, the use of mental images is God's primary paradigm for illustrating truth, both through the writers of the Bible and through Christ's use of parables.

Now there is one critical element to figurative language that you must understand. Figurative language is *fictional*.

God makes heavy use of fiction in his Word.

Not fiction as in "false or untrue," but fiction as in "not presently real."

Christ is often characterized as the Lamb of God. Does Christ actually have four legs and a fuzzy white coat of wool? Of course not.

When the Bible tells us that Christ is the Lamb of God, God is telling us to use our imaginations to connect the image of a lamb with the attributes of his Son, and to understand their similarities. God gave us our imaginations for good reason, knowing that we would need a window into the heavenly realm to understand even a fraction of the greater reality that surrounds us. He has made liberal use of literary devices that require us to use our God-given imaginations.

God's appearance has been described by a number of biblical writers, including Ezekiel, Paul, David, and John, to mention a few. Yet each vision describes him differently. Each presents a unique set of characteristics. Do any of these visions actually describe God's physical attributes? Not as far as we know. They are word pictures for our imaginations.

Examples of these word pictures are so common throughout Scripture that I'm sure you know many off the top of your head, where they have been planted as intended. The seed of David, the Lamb of God, the Lion of Judah, the eagle. All images that conjure mental associations with the truth. All fictional.

I remember being on a national television show a couple of years ago when the host asked me why I thought fiction was a good way to communicate truth. I cited the parables used by Jesus as an example of fiction to quicken understanding. To my surprise, the host corrected me on the air by insisting that all those parables actually happened and were not fictional stories at all. Naturally I begged off an argument by changing topics.

Soon after, I had just finished another national television broadcast with an unrelated party and was being driven to the airport by one of the staff when the same subject came up. Once again I was surprised by the driver's horror at my belief that the parables of Jesus were fictional stories, crafted to make a point. This time I took him to task. I do believe that by the time he dropped me off at my departure terminal, his world had been turned upside down.

I've never heard any theologian suggest that the metaphors and stories used in the Bible are anything but fictional, yet the belief seems to have found its way into the church. The problem with such faulty thinking is that it undermines the value of imagination and story, which in turn kills our dreams of heaven.

If I've challenged your understanding of how God interfaces with mankind, let me press you further. I stated early in this book that Christ's use of fiction isn't surprising considering the power of story. But there's more to the matter than the power of story. Humans have an actual *dependence* on various forms of fiction to understand truth. This is how God made us. Our minds explore all truth using the imagination first and foremost, and the imagination is quickened by metaphors and other fictional devices. Without them we often have a difficult time visualizing the truth.

Thus Christ's liberal use of fiction.

I chuckle when I hear of great leaders who spend hours each day poring over books, yet have distanced themselves from fiction. Nonsense! They engage fiction every day, particularly if they read the Bible, which makes common use of fiction. True, we don't often think in these terms, but they are hardly deniable.

As a writer of many fictional stories, I couch my convictions within the heart of full-length novels that characterize the struggle between good and evil. Not all stories attempt to dip into this struggle, but I find engaging the truth through a story tremendously useful and vital to my understanding of truth.

Words cut loose from story are powerless to affect our imaginations and, therefore, our lives. Eugene Peterson, author of *The Message*, said it best in a speech he made at the 2003 Christy Awards banquet:

> I chuckle when I hear of great leaders who spend hours each day poring over books, yet have distanced themselves from fiction. Nonsense! They engage fiction every day, particularly if they read the Bible, which makes common use of fiction.

Words amputated from stories lose accuracy, lose color and energy, congeal into god talk. They are flowers that fade and grow limp. For every theologian, we need five novelists to keep the language personally relational; for every biblical scholar we need another five novelists to keep the language participatory; for every church historian the church needs another five novelists to keep us aware that we are in the story.

Truth amputated from story is not only powerless, as Dr. Peterson pointed out, but it isn't really much truth at all. We humans require story to understand truth.

Let me once again use *The Passion of the Christ* as an example of story brought to life by imagination.

We all know the story well. In the minds of many Christians the story grew stale and was taken for granted, despite the practice of drinking Jesus' blood in the sacraments. Then came a man named Mel Gibson, who used his imagination to put flesh on the story.

Most of what we see in Gibson's vision of the passion of Christ is a product of his speculation. The grimaces, the grunts, the way the actors react to a host of situations, are all products of imagination. None are exact reenactments of what happened. We don't know how loudly Christ cried out, or what his face looked like, or what the soldiers said as they urged him up the path to his crucifixion.

But put one man's vision of what the Crucifixion must have been like on the screen, and believers weep.

We, too, need to direct our imaginations toward the stories of history and let them come alive in our minds so that our hearts may be drawn to the truth they convey. We, too, need to set our minds on the bliss that awaits us in heaven and inform our hopes of heaven with colorful images of that bliss.

Both our understanding of our own salvation history and our hope for the future depend on our imaginations.

The Discipline of Hope: Meditations

There are several practical ways to set your mind on the things of heaven so that the eyes of your heart might be opened to understanding how rich the bliss of that inheritance really is. I will address three: meditations, readings, and corporate exercises.

We are so stale in the practice of informing our imaginations about heaven that reaching beyond ourselves to do so requires a whole new way of thinking. And more than that, much, much thinking. After all, Paul didn't say, let your mind skip through the things of heaven, or occasionally glance at the things of heaven.

No, he said to *set* your mind on the things above. Much has been written on the subject of spiritual discipline, and I won't belabor the topic here. My purpose in this book is to highlight the desperate need we have of reawakening a bold and intoxicating vision of heaven. There are many existing books that delve into how we might do so. Two immediately come to mind: *The Celebration of Discipline*, by Richard Foster; and *The Way of the Heart*, by Henri Nouwen. Both are brilliant works although written very differently.

But in the end, setting one's mind on heaven is a purposeful exercise demanding use of the imagination. Find a quiet place, close your eyes to minimize distraction, and think about the most incredible experience you can imagine regarding Christ in heaven. Meditate on heaven.

If you're like many in slumber, doing this will result in a blank mind that is quickly overtaken by the concerns of this world. You become immediately discouraged and after one or two tries, you regard the whole business of meditation as an interesting

> We are so stale in the practice of informing our imaginations about heaven that reaching beyond ourselves requires a whole new way of thinking. Paul didn't tell us to occasionally glance at the things of heaven. He urged us to set our minds on the things above.

concept practiced by the more spiritual—monks and such—but not designed for you.

Be patient. Remember, this is a spiritual discipline that is totally foreign to the fallen nature.

I have been watching the Olympics as I write this book, and one race in particular caught my attention. I remember running long races as a child, and what I remember most about them is how hard they were. I can say with complete confidence that if you try to run a marathon without massive amounts of preparation, you will likely give up in the first mile or two.

Remember the many times Paul compared our lives to a race toward the finish line. Is this race won without sweat and pain? Can our efforts be successful without considerable determination?

Unlike the Olympics, our race occurs not in the body, but in the spirit and the mind. But the mind, like the body in a marathon, must be disciplined if it is to run the race toward the joy set before it. As Paul stated in his letter to the Romans, we must be transformed by the renewing of our minds (Rom. 12:2).

So let's try again. Close the book. Close your mind to the things of this world. Now meditate on running toward a brilliant beam of light. This light is bliss. Joy. Pass into its rays, and you will be swallowed by an ecstatic joy. Your whole life is really a race to get to the light set before you, after this life.

But this is just an image of our entry into heaven. What about heaven itself? The outstanding pleasure of laying eyes on Christ alone will be enough to drop you to the ground like a powerless rag doll. Have you ever experienced such strong emotion that your body ceased to function properly? Ezekiel did. John did. The fact is, in our current human state, a simple sight of God would be so overpowering that we would die, on the spot.

Imagine such raw emotion. I realize you don't normally think of heaven in these terms, but you must! Emotion is what drives us. Hope comes from the Spirit. Embrace it and enlarge your mind to grasp how rich the bliss that awaits you really is.

Some will cry idolatry at the hint of objectifying any notion of God or heaven. The purpose here isn't to worship any object but rather the very nature of God himself, made real to us through the same kinds of imagery he uses throughout his Word. God has always connected to man through the use of imagery, and there is no reason for him to stop now.

The problem with most Christians' visions of heaven is that they are terribly vague. Resist the temptation to make your vision vague. "Where there is no vision, my people perish" could easily be translated "Where there is no *clear* vision, my people perish."

So make your vision clear. Think of specifics. Images from the Word of God. From stories you've heard or read.

Pressing Out the Oil of Hope: Readings

It's very likely that your hope is uninformed because no one has ever suggested you go to such significant effort to capture an enduring vision of heaven. Certainly not an effort likened to an athlete's straining for the prize ahead. Particularly not when it comes to exercising your mind. You are more accustomed to gritting your teeth against sin. But that's not the race you run.

The race is about setting your mind on the prize.

Recall Christ's analogy in which he compared the hope for the wedding feast to oil in the ten virgins' lamps. Oil comes from where? From, among other sources, nuts and seeds.

If the oil is hope, then we must realize that pressing the oil from the seeds planted in us by the Holy Spirit is not an activity that happens all by itself. The oil has to be coaxed out with some effort. You don't throw a peanut at a bottle and end up with a jar full of peanut oil. Extracting that oil is a purposeful event. Like running a race.

So don't try to throw one or two peanuts of hope at the bottle called heaven, check for oil, and put the bottle back in a dark corner when you find no hope.

If you find no oil, then you must go about informing that hope with something that will expand your imagination of heaven. Once you have done so, you can return to meditating on a more fully informed hope.

> Don't try to throw one or two peanuts of hope at the bottle called heaven, check for oil, and put the bottle back in a dark corner when you find no hope.

I've suggested you look to the Scriptures for passages that give a glimpse into heaven and the longing we have for heaven.

Consider reading the Song of Solomon as an analogy for the bride's (the church's) desire for the Bridegroom (Christ). Here Solomon used metaphors liberally to draw out our imaginations in spectacular form.

Consider John's Revelation, filled with images of the great battle between good and evil, and the great reward, spelled out in minute detail. Whether you think of the book as a literal prophecy of the events to come or as a series of metaphors, John's Revelation overflows with figures of speech that inform our understanding of the bliss that is to come.

Consider the teaching of Jesus at the end of his ministry, when he talked about the end of the age.

Consider the glimpses that the Old Testament prophets—particularly Isaiah and Ezekiel—had of things above.

Consider heaven in all that you read between Genesis and Revelation, because in one form or another every book in the Bible points not only to the Cross, but beyond it to the joy for which it was suffered.

How many times have you read familiar passages on heaven without feeling the slightest passion for the images presented? Read them again, and this time let your mind go wild. Pretend as you read that you are there touching what John described, trembling as he did at its magnificence. You might be surprised at what you find when you free your imagination to embrace the images cast for us through Scripture.

But you should also stoke the flames of hope and desire in your heart by setting your mind on other pictures of heaven. If I were to stand at the pulpit and tell you that heaven is like a bowl of ice cream, certain images would come to your mind and, however much this simile understates heaven, you would agree to some extent, assuming you like ice cream. If I were to compare heaven to an orgasm, some of you would also agree, because the Word of God makes this allusion, but others would frown.

If I were to say that heaven is like doing two hundred miles an hour in a Viper on the autobahn, some would smile and nod their heads, and others would frown. The point is, these all are figures of speech that either will or will not connect with the reader, depending on his or her cultural context.

Let me suggest you use your God-given imagination to develop your own analogy of heaven's bliss. Feed your imagination with the analogies presented in the Word of God and deliberately connect with those images that quicken desire within your heart.

If we were created to obsess, then we must feed our obsessions with heaven, knowing that if we feed those obsessions, they will grow until we, too, can agree with Paul that dying to be with Christ is better by far.

Most descriptions of God and heaven are given through figures of speech, as I've stated. Through fictional devices, which put flesh on otherwise heady and difficult truths. I remember worshipping God early one morning while the rest of the house slept. I had a cup of coffee on my right, and I was sitting in a large overstuffed chair, reading the gospel of John.

I leaned over and pushed the play button on a CD player and began to meditate on the words to a Vineyard worship song—I can't remember which one. What I can remember is the vision that exploded in my mind at that moment. I saw God in heaven as a lake. The water of the Holy Spirit. And I imagined diving into these waters of the Holy Spirit.

A voice spoke softly in my mind: *Write this.*

And so I did write it, in a novel called *Black*.

When I tell you that God can be likened to a lamb or a lion or a bowl of ice cream or a lake, you have some understanding, but it is hardly informed. Watch what happens when you spend even a few minutes coaxing the oil of meaning from an image of heaven.

Imagine what would happen if you were to spend even more time.

The following scene won't have nearly as much meaning as it does in the flow of the novel itself, but let me try to set it up for you.

After being chased down an alley and falling from a rooftop, Thomas Hunter awakens in a reality that at first he thinks is a dream in which there is no evil. But the people around him in this "dream" reality insist that they are real, and that his experiences in the place called Denver are actually the dream.

When Hunter falls asleep in what he assumes is his dream reality, he does indeed dream of Denver. Within a matter of a few days, Thomas honestly doesn't know which reality is real and which is the dream.

Worse, he brings a real, live, deadly virus from what he thought of as the dream reality into this reality—the Denver reality. The virus goes airborne and soon threatens life as we know it on earth. Unless he and the governments that come to depend on him can find a way to stop the virus, every last human on earth will be dead in three weeks' time.

Conversely, Thomas introduces another kind of virus—evil—into the other reality. Now two worlds hang in the balance of one man's choices. At the heart of the novel we find a scene in which Thomas overcomes a terrible fear to dive into a lake filled with the Creator's presence.

Read an image of heaven fully fleshed by story, and let it press the oil of hope from your heart:

No one watching could have been prepared for what Thomas did next. In that moment, knowing what he must do—what he wanted most desperately—Tom tore his feet from the sand and sprinted for the water's edge. He didn't stop at the shore and stoop to drink as the others did. Instead he dove headlong over the bent posture of Michal and into the glowing waters. Screaming all the way.

The instant Tom hit the water, his body shook violently. A blue strobe exploded in his eyes and he knew that he was going to die. That he had entered a forbidden pool, pulled by the wrong desire, and now he would pay with his life.

The warm water engulfed him. Flutters rippled through his body and erupted into a boiling heat that knocked the wind from his lungs. The shock alone might kill him.

But he didn't die. In fact, it was pleasure that wracked his body, not death. Pleasure! The sensations coursed through his bones in great unrelenting waves.

Elyon.

How he was certain he did not know. But he knew. Elyon was in this lake with him.

Tom opened his eyes and found they did not sting. Gold light drifted by. No part of the water seemed darker than another. He lost all sense of direction. Which way was up?

The water pressed in on every inch of his body, as intense as any acid, but one that burned with pleasure instead of pain. His violent shaking gave way to a gentle trembling as he sank into the water. He opened his mouth and laughed. He wanted more, much more. He wanted to suck the water in and drink it.

Without thinking he did that. He took a great gulp and then inhaled unintentionally. The liquid hit his lungs.

Tom pulled up, panicked. Tried to clear his lungs, hacking.

Instead, he inhaled more of the water. He flailed and clawed in a direction he thought might be the surface. Was he drowning?

No. He didn't feel short of breath.

He carefully sucked more water and breathed it out slowly. Then again, deep and hard. Out with a soft whoosh.

He was breathing the water! In great heaves he was breathing the lake's intoxicating water.

Tom shrieked with laughter. He tumbled through the water, pulling his legs in close so he would roll, and then stretching them out so he thrust forward, farther into the colors surrounding him. He swam into the lake, deeper and deeper, twisting and rolling as he plummeted toward the bottom. The power contained in this lake was far greater than anything he'd ever imagined. He could hardly contain himself.

In fact he could not contain himself; he cried out with pleasure and swam deeper.

Then he heard them. Three words.

I made this.

Tom pulled himself up, frozen. No, not words. Music that spoke. Pure notes piercing his heart and mind with as much meaning as an entire book. He whipped his body around, searching for its source.

A giggle rippled through the water. Like a child now.

Tom grinned stupidly and spun around. "Elyon?" His voice was muffled, hardly a voice at all.

I made this.

The words reached into his bones and he began to tremble again. He wasn't sure if it was an actual voice, or whether he was somehow imagining it.

"What are you? Where are you?" Light floated by. Waves of pleasure continued to sweep through him. "Who are you?"

I am Elyon.
And I made you.

The words started in his mind and burned through his body like a spreading fire.

Do you like it?

Yes! Tom said. He might have spoken, he might have shouted, he didn't know. He only knew that his whole body screamed it.

Tom looked around. "Elyon?"

The voice was different now. Spoken. The music was gone. A simple, innocent question.

Do you doubt me?

In that single moment the full weight of his terrible foolishness crashed in on him like a sledgehammer. How could he have doubted this?

Tom curled into a fetal position within the bowels of the lake and began to moan.

I see you, Thomas.
I made you.
I love you.

The words washed over him, reaching into the deepest marrow of his bones, caressing each hidden synapse, flowing through every vein, as though he had been given a transfusion.

So then why do you doubt?

It was the Thomas from his dreams—from his subconscious—that filled his mind now. He had more than just doubted. That was him, wasn't it?

"I'm sorry. I'm so sorry." He thought he might die after all. "I'm sorry. I am so sorry," he moaned. "Please . . ."

Sorry? Why are you sorry?

"For everything. For . . . doubting. For ignoring . . ." Tom stopped, not sure exactly how else he had offended, only knowing that he had.

For not loving?
I love you, Thomas.

The words filled the entire lake, as though the water itself had become these words.

The water around his feet suddenly began to boil, and he felt the lake suck him deeper into itself. He gasped, pulled by a powerful current. And then he was flipped over and pushed headfirst by the same current. He opened his eyes, resigned to whatever awaited him.

A dark tunnel opened directly ahead of him, like the eye of a whirlpool. He rushed into it and the light fell away.

Pain hit him like a battering ram and he gasped for breath. He instinctively arched his back in blind panic and reached back toward the entrance of the tunnel, straining to see it, but it had closed.

He began to scream, flailing in the water, rushing deeper into the dark tunnel. Pain raged through his entire body. He felt as if his flesh had been neatly filleted and packed with salt; each organ stuffed with burning coals; his bones drilled open and filled with molten lead.

For the first time in his life, Tom wanted desperately to die.

The water forced his eyes open and images filled his mind. His mother, crying. The images came faster. Pictures of his life. A dark, terrible nature. A red-faced man was spitting obscenities with a long tongue that kept flashing from his gaping mouth like a snake's. Each time the tongue touched another person, they crumpled to the floor in a pile of bones. It was his face, he saw. Memories of lives dead and gone, but here now and dying still.

And he knew then that he had entered his own soul.

Tom's back arched so that his head neared his heels. His spine stressed to the snapping point. He couldn't stop screaming.

The tunnel suddenly gaped below him and spewed him out into soupy red water. Blood red. He sucked at the red water, filling his spent lungs.

From deep in the pit of the lake a moan began to fill his ears, replacing his own screams. Tom spun about, searching for the sound, but he found only thick red blood. The moan gained volume and grew to a wail and then a scream.

Elyon was screaming! In pain.

Tom pressed his hands to his ears and began to scream with the other, thinking now that this was worse than the dark tunnel. His body crawled with fire as though every last cell revolted at the sound. And so they should, a voice whispered in his skull. Their maker was screaming in pain!

Then he was through. Out of the red, into the green of the lake, hands still pressed firmly against his ears. Tom heard the words as if they came from within his own mind.

I love you, Thomas.

Immediately the pain was gone. Tom pulled his hands from his head and straightened out slightly in the water. He floated, too stunned to respond. Then the lake was

153

filled with a song. A song more wonderful than any song could possibly sound; a hundred thousand melodies woven into one.

I love you.
I choose you.
I rescue you.
I cherish you.

"I love you too!" Tom cried. "I choose you, I cherish you." He was sobbing, but with love. The feeling was more intense than the pain that had wracked him.

The current suddenly pulled at him again, tugging him up through the colors. His body again trembled with pleasure and he hung limp as he sped through the water. He wanted to speak, to scream and to yell and to tell the whole world that he was the luckiest man in the universe. That he was loved by Elyon, Elyon himself, with his own voice, in a lake made by him.

But the words would not come.

How long he swam through the currents of the lake he could never know. He dove into blue hues and found a deep pool of peace that numbed his body like Novocain. With the twist of his wrist he altered his course into a gold stream and trembled with waves of absolute confidence that comes only with great power and wealth. Then a turn of his head and he rushed into a red water bubbling with pleasure so great he felt himself go limp once again. Elyon laughed. And Tom laughed and dove deeper, twisting and turning.

When Elyon spoke again his voice was gentle and deep, like a purring lion.

Never leave me, Thomas.
Tell me that you'll never leave me.

"Never! Never, never, never! I will always stay with you."

Another current caught him from behind and pushed him through the water. He laughed as he rushed through the water for what seemed a very long time before breaking the surface not ten meters from the shore.

He stood on the sandy bottom and wretched a quart of water from his lungs in front of a startled Michal. He coughed twice and waded from the water. "Boy, oh boy." He couldn't think of words that would describe the experience. "Wow!"

"Elyon," Michal said. "Well, well. It *was* a bit unorthodox, diving in like that."

"How long was I under?"

Michal shrugged. "A minute. No more."

Tom slopped onto shore and dropped to his knees. "Incredible."

When you encounter this scene in the novel, you're already taking the ride with Thomas, the protagonist, and you are experiencing what he experiences. If you opened your mind just now, the same thing happened. You felt a shiver pass down your back or a lump rise in your throat. This, to me, is one of a million appropriate images of what a spoonful of heaven and hell and then heaven again must be like.

Do you see what can happen when you set your mind on things above with a fully informed imagination? There are still those among us who cry foul at such a rendering. Somehow they've picked up the absurd notion that unless a metaphor is in the holy Scriptures, it loses validity. But those same people use analogies not found in the Bible every day. They preach from the pulpit and they spin stories that make their points, because everyone knows the power of a good analogy.

But use words like *imagination* and they throw up red flags. This is precisely the same attitude that pushed the church into slumber in the first place. It is an unhealthy reaction to the corruption of imagination spawned by the devil. And now his plan has wreaked havoc with our ability to set our minds on the things above. On heaven.

I say set your mind on heaven. Liberate your imagination and connect with God, who has given you an imagination to be frequently used.

Exercising Our Hope: Corporate Exercises

Awaking from our slumber will require more than meditation; it will require more than informing our imaginations with intoxicating images of heaven. It will require activities that jolt our complacent minds into a new perspective of the bliss that awaits. I will suggest two, and let your imagination create as many as you would like.

First, it is time we began to create a greater desire in our hearts and minds for heaven through a new kind of music. Songs of the bliss that awaits us. Songs of swimming through intoxicating waters and lying prostrate before his throne, trembling with pleasure. Songs of new discoveries and no boundaries.

Songs of groaning for the day, a sickness of heart that can be healed only in that day when his presence fills us with unearthly power to create and love and bask in so many pleasures.

Music has a way of focusing our thoughts and emotions. It could be said that music is a form of raw imagination, and it is time the musicians among us flooded the airwaves and church services with songs of hope directed toward the bliss that awaits.

If you are one of those musicians, I can guarantee that when you focus your gift on the climax of your faith, you'll find a kind of emotion you may have rarely experienced in your songwriting.

Have you ever noticed how many of the old hymns speak out blatantly about heaven? "When we've been there ten thousand years, bright shining as the sun; we've no less days to sing God's praise than when we've first begun."

With some noted exceptions, heaven is now a passing reference in the few songs that do mention it. There is certainly no general obsession with heaven in our worship. If you're a writer, write songs that draw the people into a fascination for all that awaits us. The rest of us singers should sing songs that quicken our passion for heaven.

Second, we should consider ceremonies and object lessons that draw our minds to heaven. The early church celebrated Communion to remember Christ's death, and we should begin to do the same.

Many take Communion with a passing thought of Christ's death and a passing prayer of forgiveness lest they drink his blood unworthily. But have they ever *celebrated* Communion?

The early church understood Christ's admonition to take the sacraments as a celebration that ended in a banquet, much like the wedding feast that awaits us in the next life.

> Let us rejoice and be glad and give him glory! For the wedding of the Lamb has come, and his bride has made herself ready. Fine linen, bright and clean, was given her to wear . . . Blessed are those who are invited to the wedding supper of the Lamb! (Rev. 19:7–9)

The early church did not sip from tiny plastic cups in a moment of silence. They threw banquets, because the death of Christ pointed them to the great wedding banquet in the next life. The feasts even got out of hand on occasion, and Paul had to correct the Christians for drinking too much wine at these celebrations (1 Cor. 11:21).

Christ knew we would need extravagant reminders such as this to keep our minds on the memory of his death and looking forward to the day of his return. We should also liberate our minds to consider new activities that draw our minds to heaven.

If throwing a banquet at your church seems a bit over the top, then consider doing something similar in your home. Once a month go to the grocery store and buy the most delicious treats you can imagine. The best cuts of steak perhaps, or lobster, or whatever you know will be seen as truly special for the whole family. If you prefer, go to a special restaurant.

Now sit around the table and partake of this fantastic meal as a foretaste of that which is to come. Read a passage from John's Revelation, perhaps chapter 4, to awaken your hope for your inheritance and celebrate heaven. We fill our lives with celebrations of this life, such as Thanksgiving; why not celebrations for the hope that we profess?

In your church or your home group, you might consider another exercise. Many congregations light candles at Christmas and hold them high in a dark auditorium to represent Christ's light coming into the world. Wonderful. But imagine a service in which the pastor cuts the lights and speaks into the darkness. "This is our world, hidden in darkness," he says. "We, like Paul, see through a glass dimly."

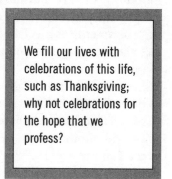

We fill our lives with celebrations of this life, such as Thanksgiving; why not celebrations for the hope that we profess?

Then the pastor lights one large candle on the stage and holds it up high. "This light," he says, "is the light of glory calling to us with a hope that exceeds all we can imagine. Set your minds now on this light. Let it draw you as flame draws the moth. Let it fill your mind and heart with a desire that brightens your world and leaves you desperate for all that will soon be yours. Even as Christ came as a Light to the world, so now the light of eternity calls us."

Let the people consider the light for a few minutes and then together sing a song of the intoxicating pleasures of heaven.

More, I would say that the congregation's attention should

be pointed to their great inheritance at every service, not with a candle necessarily, but in some way. And I would suggest that at least once a month an entire service be given to redirect our minds from this life to the life that awaits. Nothing can motivate faith like an informed hope, and nothing will inform hope but a deliberate setting of the mind.

I believe it will take these kinds of meditations and readings and songs and exercises to begin awakening most Christians from their slumber.

Once your focus has shifted from the concerns and benefits of this life and toward the bliss that awaits, you will finally find the true liberation that Christ intended for his disciples.

Then, and only then, can we take the pleasures of this life and enjoy them as foretastes of the bliss to come. We have made much of the mind and of meditation and of exercising our imaginations, but there is a great gift God has given us that fuels all of these.

For Those Who Demand a Tangible Heaven

There are bound to be readers who by this point feel at least a little dissatisfied, perhaps even cheated, by my promise to inflame their minds with visions of heaven because I've relied on such oblique devices as metaphor and analogy to do so.

But that's precisely the point, isn't it? Our vision of heaven is weak because the faculties God gave us to engage his reward are unpracticed and have slipped into slumber. Many want something physical that requires no faith. Heaven in a bottle or in a pill. But we find the heaven God has given us primarily in our hearts and minds.

Let me suggest that these devices feel inadequate only because of our own slumber. Yet it is critical that we realize these gifts are precisely what God gave us to engage him on so many levels.

We have weak visions of heaven because we have been

discouraged from using our imaginations to quicken such a vision. Instead of lamenting the fact that we see through only a glass dimly now, we should strain all the more through the lens of faith and hope to grasp how great and how wide and how deep and how rich our inheritance really is.

We should pray with Paul that the eyes of our hearts would be opened to see what is real beyond the skin of this world.

Answering Your Questions

I sometimes encounter one of two questions when I present the ideas we've just covered. The word *imagination* is so commonly associated with the enemy's camp that it stirs up all sorts of strange emotions in some people. Let me clarify by repeating my answers to your questions.

> *Where is the line drawn between metaphor/analogy/story (fiction) in the Bible and the rest of the text? What is literal, and what is figurative?*

There is a big difference between literal language and figurative language in the Bible. An example of a literal statement found in Scripture would be *God is love*. This is a direct statement that makes no use of figurative language.

An example of a figurative statement would be *Jesus Christ is the Lamb of God*. It's figurative in that Christ isn't literally a lamb; rather, he's *like* a lamb.

As we work our way through the Bible, we find many passages that employ both figurative language and literal language to characterize the overall story of God's redemption. So while one could say that the whole Bible is the true story of his redemption, the Bible uses different kinds of devices to tell that story. One of the most effective and commonly used devices is a fictional device commonly known as figurative language.

The undeniable point here is that God frequently uses fictional devices such as metaphors, analogies, and similes to communicate truth. He uses these fictional devices to help us understand the truth, because he intends to speak to us through the wonderful gift of *imagination* that he gave us. Without imagination, none of the figurative devices he employed would connect with us.

Thank God for the wonderful, expansive gift of the imagination.

> *If, as you say, we experience God primarily through our imagination that our interactions with him occur in our minds and hearts, how can we know that he is, in fact, a reality and not a figment of our imaginations?*

We *experience* God primarily through our imagination. We *know* God through our faith.

This is primarily a philosophical question that could lead us on a lengthy discourse of what it means to *know* something, a discussion we don't have the space for here. But I think it's helpful to focus on the fact that our primary interaction (experience) with God occurs beyond the five senses that we typically use to engage in our world—touch, smell, taste, sight, and hearing.

Do you taste God? Do you smell God? Do you see him? No, not usually. We taste and see that he is good with a greater faculty than our five senses. The faculty requires vision, which is nothing less than an imagined outcome. Like it or not, this is how we see God.

When we *hear* God, we usually do so with the ears of our hearts. Paul prays that the *eyes* of our hearts would be opened. These are functions of our imaginations rather than of our physical senses. We experience God in our hearts and minds far more than we do with our ears and eyes.

Why is this important? Because it implies that our experience of God can be very real, even though it may not be readily accessible to the five senses. By elevating the imagination to something as real and valuable as physical sight, for example, we elevate those experiences with God in our hearts as something just as valuable, or even more so.

In the end, however, it is our *faith* that gives us assurance that what God has spoken to our hearts really is his voice and not simply a useless figment of a wayward imagination.

Having said all of this, it turns out that God *has* bottled some of heaven for us to engage with our five physical senses. He has given us a physical representation of the bliss that awaits us. It is another one of his great gifts to us now, while we live on earth. We call this gift *pleasure*.

Let us turn our minds now to the pleasures of this life.

9

Bohemian Christianity

Embracing Pleasure on Earth

The Bohemian revolution was characterized by the unconventional and often artistic pursuit of beauty, truth, and love, ideals for all who longed for happiness; but the movement was doomed from the start, because beauty, truth, and love are impossible to find apart from God.

We have at our fingertips, however, a new Bohemian revolution that we are now at liberty to pursue. John Piper makes an eloquent argument for a kind of Christian hedonism in his book *Desiring God*. His reasoning is that we glorify God *by* enjoying him. So enjoy him and his gifts we must. We were, after all, created for this enjoyment.

We have at our fingertips, however, a new Bohemian revolution that we are now at liberty to pursue.

We have explored that wonderful, expansive gift God has given us to awaken to the pleasures of the next life, namely the imagination.

But there is another gift God has given us to awaken our passion for the next life: pleasure in this life.

The House of Delights

Picture a large house with many rooms and long wooden halls and a grassy backyard that surrounds a large blue swimming pool.

Brilliant crystal chandeliers hang over lavish spreads of food in not one but two dining rooms.

The first dining room holds the foretastes—sweet fruits and rich meats that are irresistible in every way. But these fruits and meats spoil over time and must be constantly replenished.

The second dining room holds the banquet of everlasting bliss. It's overflowing with magical-looking fruits and exotic foods that cannot spoil. The delights of this room may be seen through the windows but not eaten until the master returns to throw open the door for his banquet, which promises to make all other banquets pale in comparison.

This house is our world.

In this house there are two kinds of children. Some of the children have rejected the master's invitation to the banquet of everlasting bliss, content to gorge themselves solely on the immediate pleasures of the foretastes. They are called the children of foretastes. The second group of children are those who have accepted the master's invitation and eagerly await the banquet of bliss. They are called the children of bliss.

In the beginning, all the children tear around the house, laughing and playing with delight, splashing noisily in the pool and feasting on the lavish spreads of foretastes.

But over time, the children of bliss begin to back away from the table of foretastes because they find no lasting satisfaction in them. Indeed, the fruits and meats easily spoil and sometimes make them sick. They argue with the rest of the children, eager to set up rules for eating and playing. The master will return and satisfy them all with a far greater banquet, they cry.

But the children of foretastes loudly mock the children of bliss for ignoring such a lavish spread set before them now.

"Was not this the gift of the master?" they ask. "The master gave us these things to make us happy!"

Incensed by the wayward children's shortsightedness and their ambitious play, the children of bliss begin to avoid the children of foretastes, bringing upon themselves even more mockery.

Soon the children of bliss begin to feel like the ugly stepchild, though in reality it was for them that the master built the house. They retreat to find sanctuary from the others. They stop eating at the table of foretastes and denounce the fruits that spoil and meats that rot. They find the company of the loud children offensive, and their withdrawal is as much from the children as from the fruits and meats that spoil.

Over time the children of bliss forget what the meats and fruits left by the master taste like. And, as a result, they lose any true anticipation for the greater meats and fruits in the adjoining dining room.

In many ways, Christians have become like the children of bliss in this analogy.

While the children of our culture play noisily about the yard and swim in so many pleasures and eat from lavish spreads, we often feel like the ugly stepchild, confined to our closets, starved of the pleasures that call to us. We sneak out from time to time to nibble at the world's tables of diminished delights, then hurry back to our corners as penance for

While the children of our culture play noisily about the yard and swim in so many pleasures and eat from lavish spreads, we often feel like the ugly stepchild, confined to our closets, starved of the pleasures that call to us.

our indiscretion. Our faith quickly feels meaningless in such a small cramped space, and we soon lose all hope for any notion of victorious life.

And no wonder. We have completely forgotten about the

incredible display of fruits and meats set aside exclusively for us in the great dining room down the hall. Once, the sight of this majestic room alone was enough to make our mouths water and our bellies ache in anticipation.

But now we've rejected the foretastes of that banquet, and our hope for that great day has fallen asleep. We no longer can *remember*, much less see, the delights of that which awaits us.

The Christianity that was once our playground has somehow become a prison without hope.

The Deepest Slumber

The response of many teachers who see a church enamored by the pleasures of this world has been to drive their flock *away* from the pleasures of the world rather than *toward* the pleasures of heaven, which results in only a deeper kind of slumber, stripped of not only the pleasures of heaven but those of earth as well. This is a terrible condition that the world scoffs at, and for good reason.

I understand the reasoning behind denouncing pleasure on earth as a way to stop the hemorrhaging of sin, but doing so is contrary to God's character. God's gifts in this life are a foretaste of that which is to come. Rejecting those foretastes is tantamount to thumbing your nose at heaven. If a person is asleep to both the pleasures of this world and those of the next, it could be said he or she is in a coma.

Deep slumber.

Who could possibly be attracted to such a person? Not I, and not the lost. The lost would rather stay lost than be found in a coma.

This is no way to follow Christ. As God's children we should enjoy his feast in delight, constantly reminded that this foretaste will soon be eclipsed by pleasures we can only imagine.

And imagine them we must.

Expectations Satisfied

I began this book by saying that understanding the limitations of happiness on earth will quickly bring us closer to a fulfilled pursuit of pleasure, not drive us away from it. That when one is enamored with the bliss that awaits, he actually finds *more* pleasure here on earth, not less.

There are those who decry all pleasure, thinking that it's strictly an ugly, human thing. But God is full of pleasure. And he intends great pleasure for us not only through his gifts in this life, but more so in the life to come—what else does joy unspeakable refer to?

So let's dismiss every misguided notion that any of God's gifts are less than perfectly excellent. Let's not mock the Giver by picking holes in his offerings to us.

When one is enamored with the bliss that awaits, he actually finds more pleasure here on earth, not less.

Having said that, however, if you want to enjoy the pleasures granted us by our Creator, you first must understand how they were intended to be enjoyed and what their true purpose is. It's true that pleasure can be and often is corrupted. But it's also true that all good pleasures come from God.

In fact, when you understand that uncorrupted earthly pleasures come from God, they can fill and rejuvenate you, like that drink of water along the marathon course that urges you on to the finish. When earthly pleasures become illuminated by the light of eternity, they are far more enjoyable than when you pick away at them in the dark. The water tastes sweeter, and the meat more succulent, when you realize that after the race you will swim in the lake of his pleasure and eat at a banquet in your honor for having finished the race.

Furthermore, when you understand that earthly pleasures

are meant only as a foretaste of the indescribable pleasures that await us, your compulsion to overindulge is tempered by the realization that no particular pleasure can ultimately satisfy.

Let me use movies as an example. Like most humans on this globe, I am irresistibly drawn to a story that transports me out of my immediate surroundings into a world of new discovery.

Movies are also a form of entertainment that is clearly a kind of pleasure. I remember running eagerly to the movie theater as a young man newly discovering American culture. I was awed by the adventure in *Raiders of the Lost Ark*, swept away by the power of the fighters in *Top Gun*, moved by the loss in *Brian's Song*. I was terrified by *Aliens* and impressed by *Gandhi*. These were all hits in my mind.

> When you understand that earthly pleasures are meant only as a foretaste of the indescribable pleasures that await us, your compulsion to overindulge is tempered by the realization that no particular pleasure can ultimately satisfy.

But as I grew older, it became more and more difficult to find films that would knock my socks off. My "hit" count went from six out of every ten movies to three out of every ten movies.

If only Hollywood would get its act together and stop producing all this junk, I used to moan. But as time went by, Hollywood ignored my urgings and continued to produce junk. In fact, the more I cried foul, the more junk they seemed to produce. My hit count dropped to one out of ten. At six bucks a pop, that's sixty dollars for every good movie. No wonder the stars in Hollywood drive Mercedes.

It took some time for me to understand that Hollywood wasn't the one changing. I was. What once satisfied me no longer impressed me. My expectations for being entertained had changed. I once was thrilled by a *zap* because I had never seen a *zap*. But then I grew used to *zaps* and I wanted something else besides a *zap*.

I wanted the unexpected.

Being entertained, I began to realize, had as much to do with expectation as with raw pleasure itself. In our search for something beyond ourselves, we humans want/need/crave something new. And when we don't get it, we feel disappointed.

Consider an example from my own rearing in the jungle. Suppose you were to take a movie—any movie, regardless of how disappointed you personally might be in it—and invite a thousand locals to a natural amphitheater and show that movie on a large screen in their language. The reaction would be one of absolute wonder. Confronted by these moving pictures, they would cry out with amazement. The story would likely be the talk of the valley for weeks.

Imagine the renewed thrill we could have at every similar presentation if we were able to set aside our own expectations and become like these natives. Think how thrilling our lives would be if we could do the same with every pleasure. If we could just be like children, experiencing the wonders of God's creation in so many ways for the first time.

But we aren't like children. We've experienced all of these pleasures, and they no longer meet our expectations for a fresh engagement. We grow bored with movies. Bored with our spouses. Bored with life. Bored with God. Bored with the familiar, anemic visions we have of heaven.

They say that familiarity breeds contempt. You see it at the movies; you begin to feel it with every pleasure that once awed you.

It may take a year or twenty years or a hundred years, but eventually all our hopes for the unexpected turn into disappointments. At some point we've experienced everything that we believe we can reasonably experience. With King Solomon we lament, "There is nothing new under the sun!" Like Solomon, we search for pleasure and gather wealth and search for something new under the sun and then finally declare it all meaningless (Eccl. 1–2).

Been there, done that.

Confronted by the absence of hope for anything new, people go through stages of life called midlife crises. They trade spouses and buy faster cars and start new diets. They take part-time jobs because sitting around at home while the kids are in school no longer satisfies them. They grow bored and the boredom at first scares them, then numbs them. When they emerge from their disappointments, they've lost a portion of hope, often without realizing it until the next crisis hits.

But none of this has to be. Clearly, we can't easily wash from our minds our life experiences and engage every pleasure as if it were our first encounter with that experience, but we can do something similar.

The Cup of Raw Pleasure

We can adjust our understanding of those pleasures. We can accurately see all temporal pleasures as limited foreshadows of something coming later. For now, with pleasure as well as with knowledge, we see through only a glass dimly, but then we will see face-to-face. Now God's gifts to us are fading, but then they will be brilliant.

Each time you partake of a pleasure given to you by God, whether it be food or some form of entertainment or a treasured

> Each time you partake of a pleasure given to you by God, whether it be food or some form of entertainment or a treasured relationship, think of it as a foretaste of a much greater pleasure to come.

relationship, think of it as a foretaste of a much greater pleasure to come.

Take a glass of the finest nectar you have and pour it into a clear glass. Sip the drink, let the sweet taste linger on your tongue, and then swallow it. Now hold the glass up to the light and imagine that you have just barely tasted a drop of a far superior nectar waiting for you in another place. Let the aroma fill your nostrils, and as you do so, thank your Maker for such a gift to draw your mind to far richer pleasure at his table in the age to come.

Salute the Giver and drink deeply. This is the way to use pleasure for its intended purpose.

Let's return to the movies. Now armed with a new understanding, we go to the theater and watch a film. Our expectations of the experience have been changed. We know the movie can't be all its makers hope it will be, because anything created by man can only dimly reflect the bright light on the horizon called heaven. We watch the movie without the expectations we once had.

We watch the movie for what it really is: a creative attempt by a group of people created in God's image, trying desperately to make some sense out of their world. Or in some cases, trying to deconstruct their world. Or in still other cases, trying to poke fun at their world, and in many cases doing it all rather poorly.

Either way, you can harvest something pleasurable from nearly any creative attempt, no matter how fumbled.

What does this have to do with heaven? We should not look for any great satisfaction on earth, but in heaven alone. When you finally come to the understanding that nothing in this world can truly satisfy the thirst God has placed in you to see him face-to-face, your disappointments with this world's failure to deliver satisfaction will start to fade and you'll begin to enjoy the pleasures on this earth for what they are. Foretastes of heaven.

Your life has been burdened with the drive to find great happiness, but when you fail to find it, you either already have or will slip into a quiet dissatisfaction.

The world says that heaven is a useless figment of the imagination that can't bring happiness on earth. But they have it backward. True happiness *on earth* is the figment of our imaginations. Heaven, on the other hand, not only exists, but it's our only true source of happiness. And hope is our window into that source.

Stop trying to find total satisfaction here on earth and instead enamor your mind with heaven. Then, and only then, will you be happy here on earth. Let the burden of finding ultimate success fall from your shoulders. Rest in your inheritance. That inheritance will make the success of the highest paid entertainer or most powerful politician look silly by comparison.

And then, understanding the place of these foretastes we call pleasure, embrace them as a child might embrace them. Let your imagination draw you to the greatness behind them. Don't be driven to new pleasures by the failure of old pleasures, but be drawn to the light for which you were created.

Putting Pleasure to Use

To summarize, once we have dealt severely with our impossible expectations of this life, we can begin to relearn how to use pleasure as it was intended to be used, as a foretaste of what awaits us.

Hear me clearly: I am in no way disparaging the enjoyment of earthly pleasures. On the contrary, I think they are an important link to heaven itself. If we have no grounding in the pleasures God has given us here on earth, our minds can't connect with the analogies he's given us for heaven.

If you have never been awed by a pearl, you won't in any way be inspired by the phrase "pearly gates." I am not disparaging earthly pleasures, only our perception of them. Now we must learn to take full advantage of these gifts God has given us.

Since I've already used the movies as an example, and since

so many other pleasures raise hair on the necks of so many well-intentioned people, let's stick to the movies.

I was driving with my sixteen-year-old son the other day, and I was struck by the disparity between what we Christians say about heaven and how we feel about heaven. The disparity is something I was sure my son saw, and so I meant to drag it into the open. I wanted to help him feel some kind of real excitement for heaven.

So I leaned on one of *his* pleasures. Watching movies.

"Imagine," I said, "that *Star Trek* is real. That there really are starships flying about the universe, skipping from star system to star system, engaging a thousand different worlds. And imagine that this world is one of the worlds they have sworn not to contact for fear of interfering with humanity's progress. Can you imagine that?" I asked.

"Yes," he said.

"Good. I realize that we don't believe alien life exists, but just for the moment, let's pretend that God has allowed such life, and that he is in full control of that life. Follow?"

"Yes."

"Good. Now imagine that you were visited by an emissary who turned out to be an angel from God. The emissary whisked you away to a holding place deep in the mountains and informed you that what I've said is real. There are thousands of spaceships throughout the universe. Hundreds of exotic worlds to discover. But more than all of this, they've informed you that you are the twelfth son in a lineage that countless billions have had their eyes on for many years. You, JT Dekker, are the rightful heir to a position of great power in the universe. At this very moment more than a billion people have gathered on a certain planet in the next star system, eagerly awaiting your arrival. The time has come for you to choose to either embrace the role for which you were born or stay here on earth forever."

"Okay," my son said with a smirk.

"'You can bring seven others with you,' the emissary tells you. 'We will transport you to the planet, where you will walk into a massive arena specially built for your arrival. The roar of the crowd will shatter the stillness of space. But you have to decide today. If you choose to stay, your memory of this visit will be wiped out, and you'll never again be given the opportunity to take your rightful place as God's leader for a hundred worlds.' Follow?"

"Yes."

"Would you go?"

My son's eyes lit up. "Of course."

And what sixteen-year-old boy wouldn't? Who could resist the call of such great adventure and discovery?

"What if heaven were as real as that?" I asked. "Would you want to go? I mean now, today?"

No hesitation. "Yes."

"Heaven is more real than that. And far better," I said.

Before you start hurling the latest book to refute Mormonism at me, let me assure you, this fantasy has nothing to do with my doctrine of heaven, except that it does provide an adequate analogy for a sixteen-year-old.

If your great pleasure in life is eating ice cream, then a fantasy of diving into a huge bowl of ice cream once you die is fine by me.

If you are days from your wedding and think of heaven with the same anticipation you have for your marriage, again, that's fine by me.

No matter what the pleasure, it can provide a wonderful foretaste of something greater to come. Embrace that pleasure as a gift from God and direct your thoughts to heaven as you do. But above all, do not expect from that pleasure anything it can't deliver.

Our lives are about heaven beyond this earth, not heaven on earth.

Corrupted Pleasure

I clearly would be remiss not to discuss the corruption of pleasure at the hand of the thief who has come to steal our pleasure and bankrupt our stores of hope.

But isn't this strategy, which has received so much attention in so many books, really a transparent ploy that seems quite toothless in the light of eternity? We have been granted our inheritance as a matter of God's grace, not through any work we have done. Heaven is a gift to us. The enemy may make our lives quite miserable by robbing us of hope and rubbing our noses in sin, but when our eighty or so years on this earth end, we will see that his strategy has failed and we, the true followers of Christ, will only laugh at his desperate ploys.

Having said that, wallowing in the sin of spoiled pleasures is no fun and only detracts from the joy of hoping for heaven, so let's agree with Paul and toss spoiled pleasure aside.

There isn't a single pleasure that can't be corrupted. We think of sexual sin and drunkenness and drug addiction, but we also know that the pleasures of religion and worship and self-righteousness themselves can be offensive to God. Hear what our Maker says to his people, whom he's previously commanded to make sacrifices to him:

- When you come to appear before me, who has asked this of you, this trampling of my courts? Stop bringing meaningless offerings! Your incense is detestable to me. (Isa. 1:12–13)

- When you spread out your hands in prayer, I will hide my eyes from you; even if you offer many prayers. (Isa. 1:15)

- All of us have become like one who is unclean, and all our righteous acts are like filthy rags. (Isa. 64:6)

Humans are capable of turning anything good, including prayer, into something offensive to God. Rather than isolate specific pleasures as prone to corruption, we ought to realize that all pleasures, when not accepted as a gift from God, are corrupted.

Indeed, if there is one pleasure most prone to corruption, it isn't wine or sex or anything else that makes our top five. It's the Laodicean pleasure of slumbering safely in God's grace as recorded by John in his Revelation. Slumbering affection for God is corrupted affection, and God will spew such lukewarm affection from his mouth, as if it were spoiled water (Rev. 3:16). Here Christ admonished the church to unmask its lack of passion and realize its true state of wretchedness.

Buy "salve to put on your eyes, so you can see," he instructed (v. 18). Isn't this the same salve that we ought to buy to open the eyes of our hearts to the glory of our inheritance? What a stunning word picture.

> This is our new Bohemian revolution. Let us throw off the sin that so easily entangles and fix our minds on a relentless, unconventional pursuit of beauty, truth, and love in that place where we will come face-to-face with our Redeemer, Jesus Christ.

But those who see clearly the hope of eternity, and who passionately long for the day of their redemption, and who embrace all that God has given them, acknowledging God as the Giver of all good gifts—these he will embrace as his children.

Bohemian Christianity

This is our new Bohemian revolution. Let us throw off the sin that so easily entangles and fix our minds on an unconventional, relentless pursuit of beauty, truth, and love in that place where we will come face-to-face with our Redeemer, Jesus Christ.

Let us not shun the gifts our Creator has showered on us, but embrace them as the firstfruits of all that is to come. And let these gifts awaken our desire for the day when such pleasures will flood us like the pounding of so many unstoppable waves crashing on the shore.

Answering Your Questions

Once again a few common questions on this matter of pleasure.

> *You make several references to enjoying the extravagant pleasures here on earth, particularly through food and drink. Aren't you afraid you're promoting an irresponsible lifestyle that would lead to obesity or drunkenness?*

On the contrary, I'm promoting a lifestyle that embraces the pleasures given to us by our Creator as they were intended, rather than in a way that leads to any abuse.

Remember, the enemy has taken God's good pleasures and distorted them by offering them as a *substitute* for our true inheritance, which is heaven. The intended purpose of pleasure is to propel us down the road toward the prize, certainly not to distract us from that prize. When we overindulge in the pleasures of the flesh, we are essentially demanding ultimate satisfaction now in a way contrary to pleasure's purpose. Seeking this kind of satisfaction now is not only an impossibility this side of heaven, but it quickly becomes destructive.

Humanism has gone chasing after pleasure as an end in itself for the simple reason that it has no hope for heaven. In the same way, Christians whose hope for heaven has fallen asleep tend to either abuse pleasure or shun it altogether. But God's plan is that we partake of his pleasures as he intended: to welcome them as a foretaste of glory divine. God wants us to enjoy them as limited samples of far greater pleasures to come—seeing him face to face in glory.

Paul summed up the matter in his charge to Timothy by insisting that those who are well off in this life shouldn't put their hope in this life but in God who "richly provides us with everything for our enjoyment" (1 Tim. 6:17). Their focus should be in sharing that enjoyment with others, he says, and then he tells us why in verse 19: "In this way they will lay up treasure for themselves as a firm foundation for the *coming age* [heaven] so that they may take hold of the life that is truly life."

The things God has given us for our enjoyment in this life are good, but they are only a fraction of the true life to come.

I encourage all Christ followers to embrace God's good gifts as he intended us to embrace them—with a thankful heart and with an expansive yearning for the Giver of the gift. Did God not give us food that pleases the palette? Did he not give us beauty to look upon, and health to enjoy? Of course.

But these pleasures will corrupt if they become a substitute for the Giver of the gift.

Is there any earthly pleasure that you consider completely off-limits to the Christian?

I would consider many pleasures off limits to the Christian. In fact, I would go even further and state that any pleasure that is abused should be off limits to the follower of Christ.

The question should really be, What constitutes an abuse of pleasure? If the purpose of pleasure is to draw our hearts to the Giver of all good gifts, and we find ourselves being drawn to anything other than the Giver (who is Christ), then we abuse the gift. We use it as a substitute for glory by turning it into an earthly kind of heaven that can't possibly satisfy us and most often destroys us.

At the same time, shunning a gift from the Giver can also constitute an offense. What loving child would turn her back on a gift from her mother? By doing so, she would mock her mother. We must be careful not to mock God by degrading his good gifts to us, whatever they may be.

On a practical level, when determining what pleasures may or may not be appropriate, we should follow this simple principle: If you find pleasure in something that doesn't honor or draw you to the Giver of life, then you abuse that pleasure. Some pleasures can never honor God, and as such should always be off limits. Abusing another human being, for example. If a man finds some twisted pleasure in abusing his wife, his pleasure is born of hell, not of heaven.

If a certain presentation of food, or drink, or sex, or any other potential pleasure leads you to an offense of God (such as obesity, drunkenness, or adultery), it should be off limits. While some of these offenses are spelled out clearly in God's Word to us, others are not. In those cases, we must follow our own convictions as we prayerfully consider the guiding of the Holy Spirit for our lives.

Again, I say embrace the pleasures God has given you as a foretaste of his great inheritance that awaits you in heaven. Celebrate them. Never abuse them or allow the enemy to fool you into thinking they are more or less than what they are.

10

When Ravaging Beasts Bite

Finding Hope Past Suffering

There have been more books written on the *problem* of pain than on the joy that follows death, and it's time we set the record straight. The simple fact is that death is a problem only when it's misunderstood. Death lost its sting when Christ made a way for us to enter eternity with him. It's a problem for the slumbering and for those who have never been awake, but for those of us who have been saved into a new and living hope, bodily death is the beginning of bliss, not a problematic end. Being confronted by the death of a loved one often awakens hope in each of us. I recounted how my brother's death changed my understanding of happiness. It could be said that the problem of pain was my own salvation.

We shouldn't minimize the pain of death and suffering—they are very real and quite excruciating. Jesus wept at his friend's death. The loss of profound relationships is a difficult thing to stomach for anyone familiar with love, including God. The struggle of pain in this life is equally difficult and often unbearable.

Pain and death hurt, but that does not mean they are problematic. King Solomon clearly stated that eternity is in the heart of man. It is critical that we understand we were created for heaven, not for earth, and that our great reward will be in heaven, not on earth, and that, in fact, earth will always be replete with disappointment.

Listen to a well-stated summary of the matter by C. S. Lewis in his book *Mere Christianity*:

[Heaven] is the only thing we were made for. And there are strange, exciting hints in the Bible that when we are drawn in, a great many other things in nature will begin to come right. The bad dream will be over; it will be morning.

A bad dream? Yes, in many ways sin has turned our dreams bad. Evil has spoiled so many pleasures and introduced so many sufferings. But the redeeming work of Christ can awaken us to his intended purpose for his creation.

In so many ways our entire discussion regarding the bliss of the afterlife comes into clear focus when examined through the lens of suffering. Christianity as cast by Christ and his followers was never a faith that sought to replace the suffering we all experience in this life with an escape from that suffering on earth. Rather, it was and should be to this day a faith that makes the pain of this life inconsequential in light of the joy set before those who believe.

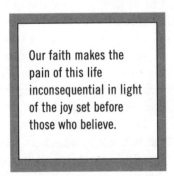

Our faith makes the pain of this life inconsequential in light of the joy set before those who believe.

You're not sure about this? Let me clarify your thinking. We are followers of Christ, are we not? Like him, we take up our crosses; like him, we set our eyes on the prize of eternal joy.

Let us fix our eyes on Jesus, the author and perfecter of our faith, who for the joy set before him endured the cross, scorning its shame, and sat down at the right hand of the throne of God. Consider him who endured such opposition from sinful men, so that you will not grow weary and lose heart. (Heb. 12:2–3)

Why did Christ endure the Cross? For *joy*, that treasured emotion set before him at the right hand of the throne of God! We should remember the joy set before Christ so that when we suffer we don't lose heart. We, too, as his followers, are destined for that joy.

> Why did Christ endure the Cross? For joy, that treasured emotion set before him at the right hand of the throne of God!

How can we remember that joy set before Christ if we have no clear understanding of it? you ask.

But we do! If the eyes of our hearts are opened and we set our minds on the climax of our story, we can have a clear understanding of paradise. We will have to use the many metaphors cast for us in the Word, and we will have to use that incredible gift graciously given to us by our Maker—the imagination—but by doing so we can fill our minds with a vision of the bliss to come.

This is our vision, without which we will perish. Using Bill Hybel's definition of *vision*, we must form a "picture of the future that produces passion." We must envision the coming riches of heaven in many wonderful, intoxicating ways, and then we must place our hope in the riches of that inheritance.

The writer of Hebrews went on to tell his readers that they haven't yet suffered to the point of shedding blood, so they should be grateful. What odd words of encouragement from this early church leader. Certainly not seeker-sensitive. Yet in the context of the early church's obsession with the afterlife, these words of encouragement make perfect sense.

In today's Christian culture we would expect to hear other words: *Keep praying and seeking and living holy lives so that you will escape any suffering headed your way. And by the way, if you want to turn financial hardship into happy, snappy times, you should up your giving.*

A far cry from Paul's kind of encouragement, don't you think?

Jesus told his followers that they should expect suffering,

not as a result of any failing or lack of belief on their part, but specifically because they followed him. Consider:

If they [the world] persecuted me, they will persecute you also. (John 15:20)

And on another occasion, speaking about the end times:

Brother will betray brother to death, and a father his child; children will rebel against their parents and have them put to death. All men will hate you because of me, but he who stands firm to the end will be saved. When you are persecuted in one place, flee to another. (Matt. 10:21–23)

Yet Christianity's fixation on the benefits and comforts of this world has diverted complete attention from the true benefit of our faith—the bliss of the afterlife, heaven, which is better *by far* than this life.

Going One Step Further

The hope of that which is to come isn't merely an anesthetic to help us bear our burdens here on earth. The pain of suffering, which is actually an integral part of our faith, sets our minds on things above.

If pleasure is given to draw us to greater pleasures to come, then suffering is allowed to prod us toward the same objective.

Imagine with me a sleeping man snoring loudly in bed. In a state of panic (the cause of which we won't concern ourselves with), you rush into the room, desperate to wake this slumbering man from his sleep. Several ideas flash through your head.

You yell, but the man sleeps on. *Water*, you think. *I'll dump a bucket of water on his head.* But you have no water.

What you do have is a pocketknife, and it happens to be in

your hand. This is your sword of truth. You run to the bed and jab the knife into the man's thigh.

Ouch!

Our man's nerves are working better than his ears, and to say he awakes is an understatement. The man not only finds himself instantly and fully aware, but he awakes with a roar and arches his back as if jolted by a strong electrical current.

This, my friends, is an awakening from slumber.

I'm not suggesting we swing our pocketknives of truth around every room we enter, hoping to puncture the flesh of any soul who happens to get in our way. I'm only illustrating pain's ability to gather attention.

This is essentially how the pain of my brother's death jolted me from my own slumber.

This is how death and suffering prod us to reexamine our perspectives of the afterlife.

An absurd example? Perhaps, but it isn't terribly different from what rises from between the lines of Paul's confession to the Philippians:

> I want to know Christ and the power of his resurrection and the fellowship of sharing in his sufferings, becoming like him in his death, and so, somehow, to attain to the resurrection from the dead. (3:10–11)

Stop. The statement, though often repeated, is clearly foreign in today's Christian culture. Today, Christianity is obsessed with employing the power of Christ to escape any kind of pain and with extending this life until we are finally forced to enter the afterlife rather than obtaining resurrection, as Paul stated.

But this was Paul, the man obsessed with the afterlife. The man who considered dying and being with Christ better *by far* than enjoying life on this earth. Yet Paul went even further in explaining this strong tie between life and death:

Not that I have already obtained all this [death and resurrection of the dead], or have already been made perfect, but I press on to take hold of that for which Christ Jesus took hold of me. Brothers, I do not consider myself yet to have taken hold of it. But one thing I do: Forgetting what is behind and straining toward what is ahead, I press on toward the goal to win the prize for which God has called me heavenward in Christ Jesus.

All of us who are mature should take such a view of things. (vv. 12–15)

Once again Paul talked about our journey of faith in terms of pressing and straining toward the great reward of heaven, as a runner might press toward the finish line. Not only does the suffering of this world seem insignificant so as to be *forgotten* by him, but that suffering seems to actually be *part* of his goal! He, like Christ, embraced the pain of physical death for the reward set before him.

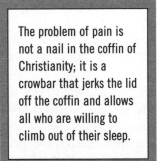

The problem of pain is not a nail in the coffin of Christianity; it is a crowbar that jerks the lid off the coffin and allows all who are willing to climb out of their sleep.

The problem of pain is not a nail in the coffin of Christianity; it is a crowbar that jerks the lid off the coffin and allows all who are willing to climb out of their sleep.

Now, this is all well and good unless you are at this moment suffering for your faith or experiencing the excruciating pain of illness or death. I am confronted now with this bladder business that I've written about. I am living through a period of suffering now. I have pain, and I have concern over my future. But this condition draws my mind to things beyond this life.

I don't make light of suffering, but considering the words of Christ and Paul, I am eager to put that suffering in the balance of life everlasting.

I mentioned earlier that my daughter Chelise was recently diagnosed with JMDS, an incurable skin disease. We were distraught with worry for her. But Chelise, a child like the children whom Jesus urged his disciples to emulate, wasn't so concerned. She had difficulty climbing stairs, and she no longer could dance around the living room as she once had. But tell Chelise that she was sick and she would only roll her eyes.

"I'm not sick, silly," she would say. "I only have a disease!"

In her young believing mind, this ailment was only a passing inconvenience called disease. When the doctor prescribed large doses of prednisone to settle her immune system, she gathered the family with great pride, showing how she could swallow the pills without water. She couldn't skip around the coffee table because of her pain, but she could still sing the same endless, make-believe songs that she always had.

Her condition has improved tremendously since that day several months ago, and the disease is expected to go into complete remission within two years. It will be a long battle, but our hope is strong.

Let me encourage you with a few thoughts. First of all, pain is but a passing phase. If only we can accept this with the same simple faith a child demonstrates.

Having said that, the pain we suffer on earth is here to stay for a while. Sadly, since the dawning of the seeker-sensitive movement, the church has sold many tired, longing souls escapism in the here and now without holding up the truth that our escape is on the other side of the finish line. Like a salesman who tries to sell race cars without engines in them. Suffering is an intricate part of the engine of our faith, meant to drive us toward the finish line.

Paul never tried to escape the pain while alive, only to use it for his race toward eternity. The saying may be a bit crass for this topic, but "no pain, no gain" seems to fit Paul's theology well. Christ suffered *pain* for the *gain* of what lay before him.

Paul considered participating in the *pain* of death a small price to pay for the *gain* of knowing Christ in his suffering and resurrection. Christ in heaven.

As we strain toward the prize, our bodies will ache and our lungs will burn. But *because* of that pain we will groan inwardly with all of creation for the day when that pain will be gone forever. There are no words that can possibly take that pain away. There are only words that can change the way we understand the pain.

In the meantime, we, like my daughter and Paul, ought to keep our minds firmly fixed on the adventure and prize set before us. Our minds should be set on bliss. We must inflame our hope for our great reward by informing that hope with the tangible pleasures of heaven. We must obsess after Christ and the power of his resurrection. Preoccupy our minds with our inheritance.

> We should obsess after Christ and the power of his resurrection. We should preoccupy our minds with our inheritance. Otherwise, our pain will rage unchecked and will bear a fruit of bitterness and hopelessness.

If we can do none of these, our pain will rage unchecked and will bear a fruit of bitterness and hopelessness.

Hope, the Sum of Suffering

Earlier, I mentioned a comment Paul made to the Romans that now has new relevance. Listen:

> We rejoice in the hope of the glory of God. Not only so, but we also rejoice in our sufferings, because we know that suffering produces perseverance; perseverance, character; and character, hope. And hope does not disappoint us. (Rom. 5:2–5)

Here Paul firmly connected the suffering of this life as a necessary part of our race to the finish line. His assertion that we should rejoice in suffering is over the top in today's Christian culture, but not in the Christianity founded by Christ.

Particularly interesting about his comment is the progression that Paul set up. He started off with the chief objective of our faith—our hope of the glory of God. This is the finish line, so to speak.

Then he moved directly to suffering, which is part of the true Christian's race. *Suffering* is important because it leads to *perseverance*, he said.

Perseverance, then, when it has been plied and tested, develops *character* along the course. It's what drives the marathon runner over the course.

Then comes the most surprising part of Paul's progression. The grand prize isn't character, but something that follows character.

Hope.

If character is elusive among humans, hope is even harder to find unless the eyes of our hearts are opened. Hope is greater than perseverance and character because it points us to our goal, lest we run our race in vain. As such, it has become the choice target of all those forces aligned against us.

It's no wonder that Christianity has fallen asleep to this most elusive, wonderful gift called hope.

It's amazing that at the end of suffering and perseverance and character we are presented with desire. An emotion. Why? Because it was no secret, even two thousand years ago, that humans are primarily motivated by emotion.

Even more amazing is Paul's assertion in Colossians 1:5, which claims that both faith and love spring from hope. Put his letter to the Romans together with his letter to the Colossians and you find the following progression: Suffering gives us perseverance; perseverance gives us character; character gives us hope; out of hope spring faith and love.

Hope, my friends. It's all about hope.

The Final Report—For Now

I went to the doctor today. He examined me—another painful experience. No spot.

It seems I don't have cancer after all. Short of an accident, I won't be dying anytime soon. Oddly, I'm not as thrilled as I assumed I would be. Strange how we take our health for granted. Does it really matter that much either way?

A Mad, Mad Delight

There is a story about a priest whose eyes were opened to the hope of delight beyond the skin of this world. I think a quick immersion in that story will demonstrate all that I have been saying about the delight that awaits us.

The Martyr's Song (Nashville: WestBow Press, 2005) is a novella born of my own search for hope following my brother's death. Parts of it were published in *When Heaven Weeps* in 2001, but now a new vision of that story captures the heart of hope. I've never written a story that drained me of tears as this one did. I sat at my computer, typing the story as it came to me, and the screen was blurry, and my cheeks were wet, and I had to stop often to gain composure.

My emotions ran circles around hope, occasionally dipping into the core of that sentiment for a raw dose that started my fingers trembling. I can't think of a better way to honor the hope we have in Christ than to test it against its greatest adversary, death.

The Martyr's Song is set in Bosnia, near the end of World War II. Father Michael is a gentle, loving man with great insight, who shepherds peaceful people committed to serving God in their small village. But one day a bitter commander who has no love for Christians comes upon the valley with his ragged troop of soldiers. The commander leads his soldiers into the village, where they encounter the entire village gathered for a young girl's birthday party. He is confronted by a love that he can't rightly grasp.

Enraged by the display of love and faith in a world gone mad, the commander determines to turn the village into a graveyard full of martyrs. But here, in the heart of horror, a hope springs eternal:

Father Michael remembered arguing with the commander; remembered the children whimpering; remembered Karadzic's rifle butt smashing down on sister Marie's skull; remembered the other soldier—the skinny one—raising his rifle to strike him. He even remembered closing his eyes against that first blow to his kidneys. But with that blow, the strobe had ignited in his mind again.

Poof!

The courtyard vanished.

The world changed for the second time that day. A brilliant flash ignited in his mind, as if someone had taken a picture with one of those flashbulbs that popped and burned out. Father Michael's body jerked and he snapped his eyes open. He might have gasped, he didn't know because this world with all of its soldiers and crying children and trudging women was too distant to judge accurately.

In its place stretched a white horizon, flooded with streaming light.

And music.

Faint, but clear. Long, pure notes, the same as he'd heard earlier. A song of love.

Michael shifted his gaze to the horizon and squinted. The landscape was endless and flat like a huge desert, but covered with white flowers. Light streamed several hundred feet above the ground toward him from the distant horizon.

A tiny wedge of alarm struck the base of Michael's spine.

He was alone in this white field. Except for the light, of course. The light and the music.

He could suddenly hear more in the music. At first he thought it might be the spring, bubbling back in the courtyard. But it wasn't water. It was a sound made by a child. It was a child's distant laughter! And it was rushing toward him from that far horizon, carried on the swelling notes of music.

Gooseflesh rippled over Michael's skin. He suddenly felt as though he might be floating, swept off his feet by a deep note that he could feel to his bones.

The music grew and with it the children's laughter. High peals of laughter and giggles, not from one child, but from a hundred children. Maybe a thousand children or a million, swirling around him now from every direction. Laughter of delight, as though from a small boy being mercilessly tickled by his father. Then reprieves followed by sighs of contentment as others took up the laughing.

Michael could not help the giggle that bubbled in his own chest and slipped out in short bursts. The sound was thoroughly intoxicating. But where were the children?

A single tone suddenly reached through the music. A man's voice, pure and clear, with the power to melt whatever it touched. Michael stared out at the field where the sound came from.

A man was walking his way, a shimmering figure, still only an inch tall on the horizon. The voice belonged to this man. He hummed a simple melody, but it flowed over Michael with intoxicating power. The melody started low and rose through the scale and then paused. Immediately the children's laughter swelled, responding directly to the man's song. He began again and the giggles quieted a little and then swelled at the end of this simple refrain. It was like a game.

Michael's humped shoulders were now shaking with silly strings of laughter. *Oh, my Father, what's happening to me?*

I'm losing my mind. Who was this minstrel walking toward him? And what kind of song was this that made him want to fly with all those children whom he could not see? Michael bent his head back and searched the skies for children. Come out, come out wherever you are, my children. Were they his children? He had no children.

But now he craved them. *These* children, laughing around him. He wanted these children—to hold them; to kiss them; to run his fingers through their hair and roll on the ground, laughing with them. To sing this song to them.

He reached up and touched the edge of the light streaming overhead. A warmth flooded his bones and he very nearly dropped to his knees with shock. His heart was suddenly pounding and he desperately wanted to step into this light. If only he could step . . .

The flashbulb ignited again. *Pop!*

The laughter evaporated. The song was gone.

It took only a moment for Father Michael to register the simple, undeniable fact that he was once again standing on the steps of his church, facing a courtyard filled with women who slumped heavy crosses over cold, flat concrete. His mouth lay open, but he seemed to have forgotten how to use the muscles in his jaw.

The commander glared at him. "You laugh? Are you mad?"

The Martyr's Song personifies all the intoxicating bliss we've discussed in a story that puts flesh to dogma.

If we could only see what truly lies behind the skin of this world. If we could peek into heaven and gape in awe at the mind-bending bliss that awaits. We would beg with Paul for entry at the earliest possible opportunity. We would gather our loved ones and demand that they fill their lamps with oil and set out for the great wedding feast in the sky.

And would we talk about what we had seen? With the

exuberance of a newly born believer. Like fools, bouncing off the walls in our excitement. If the world thinks of us as strangers now, imagine how they would characterize us upon our describing that mansion awaiting in the sky!

They would certainly certify us mad.

If only we could see, we could all lay down the sin that so easily enslaves us, embrace a deep desire for our inheritance, and live happily, madly together.

But we can see. We can! Not with this set of round organs above the nose called eyes, but with those set deep in our hearts and minds.

> Do you want to be happy? Then dive into a deep lake of hope and drink a spoonful of ecstasy. See the face of God with the eyes of your heart, and crave him more.

With the eyes of the heart. We can see, and we must if we want to embrace the hope we have in our Savior and the riches of the glorious inheritance we have in him.

So, then, infatuate yourself with this hope. Don't try to beat happiness out of this life, but embrace the life God has given you, no matter what kind of suffering comes your way. For suffering will produce perseverance, and perseverance will produce character, and character will produce hope.

And hope will not disappoint.

Do you want to be happy? Then dive into a deep lake of hope and drink a spoonful of ecstasy. See the face of God with the eyes of your heart, and crave him more.

Obsess after him. Preoccupy your mind with the things above, where Christ is seated at the right hand of God.

Groan for the day of your wedding. Weep with patience for that day of your inexhaustible pleasure. Long for him.

Wake from your slumber and embrace hope.

Answering Your Questions

Naturally some of you will have questions regarding suffering. The problem of pain has dogged people of faith for all of time. Well then, here we go—some answers in light of the slumber of Christianity.

> *What possible reason could there be for God allowing small children to suffer and be abused, and how does this kind of suffering lead anyone to a hope for heaven?*

Clearly the mere thought of a child's abuse sends shivers of horror through us all. In my understanding of God's Word there is no difference between the suffering of an innocent child and the suffering of the early Christians who were made innocent through the shed blood of Christ. We tend to empathize with one group more than the other, but in God's eyes they are the same. In both cases his precious children are being abused.

So then the question is clearer if we ask why God would allow suffering to any of those he loves, and how such suffering can possibly lead one to a hope for heaven.

In regards to the first part of the question, suffering is simply an extension of evil. By allowing evil, God allows suffering. Why does he allow evil? The short answer is that he created us with a free will to chose between two diametrically opposed alternatives. A choice between good and evil, not good and good. Anything less wouldn't really be a choice at all. In creating us in his image, God opened up a choice based on our free will. By choosing against him, we choose evil, the substance of that choice. So evil exists because we exists, created in the image of God with free will.

The long answer would require another book, so I'll leave it alone for now.

As for how suffering can lead to hope, the answer in the Scriptures is quite simple: In the same way that pleasure draws us, pain pushes us. Although pain is not God's design, our deliverance from pain is. We are being saved from death to life. From hell to heaven. From suffering on this earth, which has been defiled by sin, to sinless bliss in heaven.

It is impossible to read the New Testament and not see that the early church was consumed with the thought that their inheritance in heaven represented, among other things, an escape from the pains of this world. To the extent that heaven will be free of pain, we have hope for that day.

> *Do you think it is easier for a man who has experienced many earthly pleasures (foretastes of glory) to have a genuine hope for heaven than for a man who has experienced great suffering and torment here on earth?*

No. I think that pain is a greater force than pleasure for motivation. I also think that most of those who have experienced many earthly pleasures have done so by abusing them and turning pleasure into a kind of earthly heaven. Doing so only spoils the gift and leaves the senses deadened to the purpose of the pleasures.

Abuse of God's gifts never leads to God.

It seems that those who have been saved from lives of torment tend to have a greater appreciation for their salvation. But those who have lived in abusive situations and been subjected to great pain can also have a hard time understanding or accepting God's mercy. The bottom line is that neither the abuse of pleasure nor suffering are part of God's design. He can and does save us from both, though. In the end, heaven will be a filled with pleasure and absent of pain.

> *What would you say to a Christian who suffers from clinical depression or anxiety, who often feels without hope?*

I would say that he suffers first and foremost from the terrible slumber of Christianity. Whether his lack of hope is motivated by a clinical condition, or bad doctrine, or weak faith, his hope for heaven is in slumber.

Characterizing the problem in these terms focuses this question: How do those who suffer from depression awaken to a great hope for heaven?

The only advice I can offer might seem naive to some, but I believe it's the truth of the matter: Immerse yourself in the hope of heaven.

Read books on the coming of Christ. Read the many, many passages in the Word of God that flood the mind with hope. Obsess yourself with a day soon coming that will sweep you into your inheritance. Naturally you won't feel that hope at first, but trust me, you were created for it. Your mind and body and spirit crave it more than any drug. Your mind will quickly catch up with the discipline you exercise in inflaming hope.

The problem with depression is that when we struggle with it, we have no motivation to discipline our minds and spirits. Instead we want to sleep. Our slumber is perpetuated by a need to escape into sleep.

The first step to awakening may be physiological—perhaps even clinical. But in the end, the hope for eternity can only be awakened by the Holy Spirit when you willfully set your mind on the hope of heaven.

> *Do you believe that the medical community is taking too many strides in prolonging life, for example, through experimental drugs, radiation, chemotherapy?*

Medicine is one of God's gifts to us while we live in a diseased world. In the same way that Paul urged Timothy to drink some wine for his stomach problems (1 Tim. 5:23), I would urge people to take aspirin for pain when it makes sense to do so. Both the wine that Paul prescribed and the aspirin that a doctor might prescribe today are man-made—but from God-created elements.

Is there really any difference between these man-made remedies and bone graphs or radiation treatment or various medicines? I don't think so. Nursing health is a good thing, and by extension so is extending life, because nursing someone who is sick back to health, no matter what her age, is extending her life. Clearly, Paul thought that the extension of life was a good thing, or he wouldn't have urged his friend to take care of his health.

The real question we should ask ourselves is *why* we want to extend our lives. Is it because we have no passion for the afterlife? If so, we have a problem. Is it because, despite our desire to be with Christ, we feel there is more that God would have us do here? Then I think, like Paul, we are on solid footing.

11

What Now

Tell Me How I Should Live

Now at the end of our journey of discovery, there are still some who are grappling with the ideas presented in this book. You agree with me for the most part, but you would like just a little bit more to be won over, so to speak. Just a little bit more so that you can tie a bow on it and call it good.

Honestly, I don't feel compelled to win anyone over. I do, however, feel compelled to wake a few people up from the slumber of Christianity. The lack of passion for the inheritance that God has promised his children in the next life is quite obvious and troubling to say the least. If you don't see that in your corner of the world, you are probably dead asleep. Either that, or in a very unique corner, to be sure.

This book details that lack of passion, and labels it a slumber which has lulled millions of Christians to sleep. So then we can agree, it's quite clear that the church today has little passion for the coming life. The questions that must be answered are 1) How did we come to this place of slumber, and, 2) how can we wake to a new and living hope for all that God has prepared for his bride.

I detailed the first point, how we came to this place, in the first four chapters. In many ways the enemy has tricked us. In other ways our own religion has fooled us. Still in other ways, our own fallen nature seems determined to ignore the voice of

Christ calling us home. I surely didn't cover all of the possibilities of how we came to be in this slumber — you may have some excellent thoughts of your own. Either way, I doubt you need much convincing that we are indeed here.

This brings us to the second question, how one wakes to a new and living hope. I believe it is a matter of renewing our minds. Hope springs from faith and so we must believe. But there are a number of practical ways to inflame that hope, among them the following: 1) We should also intentionally set our minds on heaven. 2) We should enjoy pleasure as it was intended because it *draws* us to heaven. 3) We should allow the pain that comes our way to *push* us into our Creator's arms. 4) Because our hope is made real by a fully fleshed vision of a reality that awaits just beyond this one, we should fan that vision to life through song and readings and meditation. Without that vision, God's people perish. With it we, like Paul, thrive on a deep desire to be with Christ in glory, a place we can now only imagine. Because we can only imagine heaven, we must imagine it.

In a very small nutshell, there you have it.

Many Christians want a more tangible teaching to guide their lives. They want specific steps to drive them down a road. Here and now realities that they can touch and see and hear with their five senses. Tell me specifically what I should do? they ask.

But the simple truth of the matter is that our faith isn't first about what you do, but about what you believe. What you do will flow from what you believe. Belief isn't found in five steps for dynamic living or in any of the popular self help books that fill our shelves. Indeed, our obsession with the tangible has enabled our Slumber.

In reality, our faith comes by hearing the word of God with our hearts.

By thinking on things above.

By emptying our lives of useless things and filling them with ideas of our Maker.

By being a child and enjoying our Father's pleasure while yearning to be with him.

By majoring on the heart, the mind, and the soul which will yield a work that is not dead.

How should you live now, you ask? You should acknowledge your true condition, whatever that is. Then you should fix your mind on the truth.

The truth of heaven. The truth that this life will quickly pass and the staggering reality of the life to come will be upon us. The truth that you were created for that life more than for this life. Thinking on these matters alone will begin to change everything you do.

Fixing your mind on heaven will change your life on earth. You really don't need more from me at this point. Begin here and let the truths of this book fill your heart, mind and soul. Perhaps in another book we can discuss the things we should do while we think on these things, but to do so now would only undermine the importance of first awakening to truth.

As I look across the landscape of the church I see many leaders and movements trumpeting the same message. The Holy Spirit frequently speaks the same message to many of his children. It seems he has done so now. By writing this book I join with all of the other voices crying in this sleepy wilderness:

Wake. Wake O Sleeper.
Open the eyes of your heart to the bliss set before you
Run your race with your eyes fixed on the goal
Embrace God; embrace love; embrace hope
Preoccupy your mind and heart with Christ in Glory
Wake, Bride of Christ, wake. The wedding feast is coming soon.

DEAR READER:

I've written a short novella called *The Martyr's Song* that personifies the journey of happiness that we've discussed in *The Slumber of Christianity* in a way that simply isn't possible without story. It's one thing to know that you long to be happy now while you wait for heaven. It's another thing to experience an awakening that truly changes your life. Story allows you to experience a journey with a character in a way that nonfiction can only suggest.

I strongly urge you to read *The Martyr's Song.* Take a journey into the power of hope that will alter the way you look at both this life and the next. Then, having done so, ask yourself once again what you should do to be happy in this life. Included with the book is a song written and performed by Todd Agnew. It was written exclusively for this story which will awaken your passion for heaven on earth.

Ted Dekker